Working with Static Sites
Bringing the Power of Simplicity to Modern Sites

Raymond Camden and Brian Rinaldi

Beijing · Boston · Farnham · Sebastopol · Tokyo  O'REILLY®

Working with Static Sites

by Raymond Camden and Brian Rinaldi

Printed in the United States of America.

Published by O'Reilly Media, Inc., 1005 Gravenstein Highway North, Sebastopol, CA 95472.

O'Reilly books may be purchased for educational, business, or sales promotional use. Online editions are also available for most titles (*http://oreilly.com/safari*). For more information, contact our corporate/institutional sales department: 800-998-9938 or *corporate@oreilly.com*.

Editor: Allyson MacDonald	**Indexer:** Wendy Catalano
Production Editor: Shiny Kalapurakkel	**Interior Designer:** David Futato
Copyeditor: Gillian McGarvey	**Cover Designer:** Karen Montgomery
Proofreader: Susan Moritz	**Illustrator:** Rebecca Demarest

March 2017: First Edition

Revision History for the First Edition
2017-02-28:   First Release

See *http://oreilly.com/catalog/errata.csp?isbn=9781491960943* for release details.

978-1-491-96094-3

[LSI]

Table of Contents

Preface

Over the past few years, static site generators have gone from being a bit of a novelty only the über-geeks used to prove the quality of their skill, to becoming widely used tools that power a large and growing part of the internet. Because of the benefits they offer, static site generators are now used to run thousands of sites and are becoming the basis for a broad set of tools that even reach the casual developer and even the nontechnical content writer.

Still, the static site ecosystem is still young and slightly immature, meaning that it can be difficult to know which tools to choose and how to get started. That is the problem we hoped to address in writing this book. By providing common scenarios and insights on how to address them, we hope to make it easier for anyone—from the experienced web expert to the beginning web developer—to create static site solutions and take advantage of the speed, flexibility, and security that they offer.

What You Need to Know

Is this book for you? The following items can help you determine that:

Who this book is for

This book is for web developers who are looking for a simpler way to build and deploy websites. For developers with experience with dynamic app servers (like PHP, Node.js, and ColdFusion), this book will present a simpler alternative. For developers who are still working with simple websites but need a way to make them more powerful, this could be just the ticket to bringing your sites to the next level.

What's not covered

This book focuses on static site generators that work from the command line. Desktop tools that have similar features are not covered.

How this book is organized

The book begins by describing why you would want to use static sites. Each subsequent chapter focuses on a specific type of site and uses this as a way of introducing different static site generators.

After discussing how to build a site, the book moves on to cover more advanced topics such as adding dynamic elements back in, working with a CMS, and how to deploy and host your static site.

The last chapter discusses how to migrate from a dynamic site to a static one.

Conventions Used in This Book

The following typographical conventions are used in this book:

Italic
> Indicates new terms, URLs, email addresses, filenames, and file extensions.

`Constant width`
> Used for program listings, as well as within paragraphs to refer to program elements such as variable or function names, databases, data types, environment variables, statements, and keywords.

`Constant width bold`
> Shows commands or other text that should be typed literally by the user.

`Constant width italic`
> Shows text that should be replaced with user-supplied values or by values determined by context.

This element signifies a tip or suggestion.

This element signifies a general note.

This element indicates a warning or caution.

Using Code Examples

Supplemental material (code examples, exercises, etc.) is available for download at *https://github.com/cfjedimaster/Static-Sites-Book*.

This book is here to help you get your job done. In general, if example code is offered with this book, you may use it in your programs and documentation. You do not need to contact us for permission unless you're reproducing a significant portion of the code. For example, writing a program that uses several chunks of code from this book does not require permission. Selling or distributing a CD-ROM of examples from O'Reilly books does require permission. Answering a question by citing this book and quoting example code does not require permission. Incorporating a signifi-cant amount of example code from this book into your product's documentation does require permission.

We appreciate, but do not require, attribution. An attribution usually includes the title, author, publisher, and ISBN. For example: "*Working with Static Sites* by Ray-mond Camden and Brian Rinaldi (O'Reilly). Copyright 2017 Raymond Camden and Brian Rinaldi, 978-1-491-96094-3."

If you feel your use of code examples falls outside fair use or the permission given above, feel free to contact us at *permissions@oreilly.com*.

O'Reilly Safari

 *Safari* (formerly Safari Books Online) is a membership-based training and reference platform for enterprise, government, educators, and individuals.

Members have access to thousands of books, training videos, Learning Paths, interac-tive tutorials, and curated playlists from over 250 publishers, including O'Reilly Media, Harvard Business Review, Prentice Hall Professional, Addison-Wesley Profes-sional, Microsoft Press, Sams, Que, Peachpit Press, Adobe, Focal Press, Cisco Press, John Wiley & Sons, Syngress, Morgan Kaufmann, IBM Redbooks, Packt, Adobe Press, FT Press, Apress, Manning, New Riders, McGraw-Hill, Jones & Bartlett, and Course Technology, among others.

For more information, please visit *http://oreilly.com/safari*.

How to Contact Us

Please address comments and questions concerning this book to the publisher:

O'Reilly Media, Inc.
1005 Gravenstein Highway North
Sebastopol, CA 95472
800-998-9938 (in the United States or Canada)
707-829-0515 (international or local)
707-829-0104 (fax)

We have a web page for this book, where we list errata, examples, and any additional information. You can access this page at *http://www.oreilly.com/catalog/0636920051879.do*.

To comment or ask technical questions about this book, send email to *bookquestions@oreilly.com*.

For more information about our books, courses, conferences, and news, see our website at *http://www.oreilly.com*.

Find us on Facebook: *http://facebook.com/oreilly*

Follow us on Twitter: *http://twitter.com/oreillymedia*

Watch us on YouTube: *http://www.youtube.com/oreillymedia*

Acknowledgments

From Raymond Camden:

First and foremost—I thank my wife. Jeanne, you always believe in me and always support me. Thank you.

Second, thank you, Brian, for agreeing to write with me. While we may be mortal enemies, I'm happy we were able to put our differences aside for this endeavor! ;)

Lastly, thank you to everyone who reads, and participates, at my blog (raymondcamden.com). Your questions and comments keep me on my toes!

From Brian Rinaldi:

I'd like to thank my wife, Claudia, whose love and support makes me a better man.

I'd like to thank Ray for proposing this book in the first place and for constantly pushing me to actually finish it. Now that this is over, I will resume planning his destruction.

## CHAPTER 1

Why Static Sites?

Brian Rinaldi

In the beginning, the web only consisted of static sites. In fact, the first website (*http://info.cern.ch/hypertext/WWW/TheProject.html*), created on August 6, 1991, and shown in Figure 1-1 was (and still is) technically a static site.

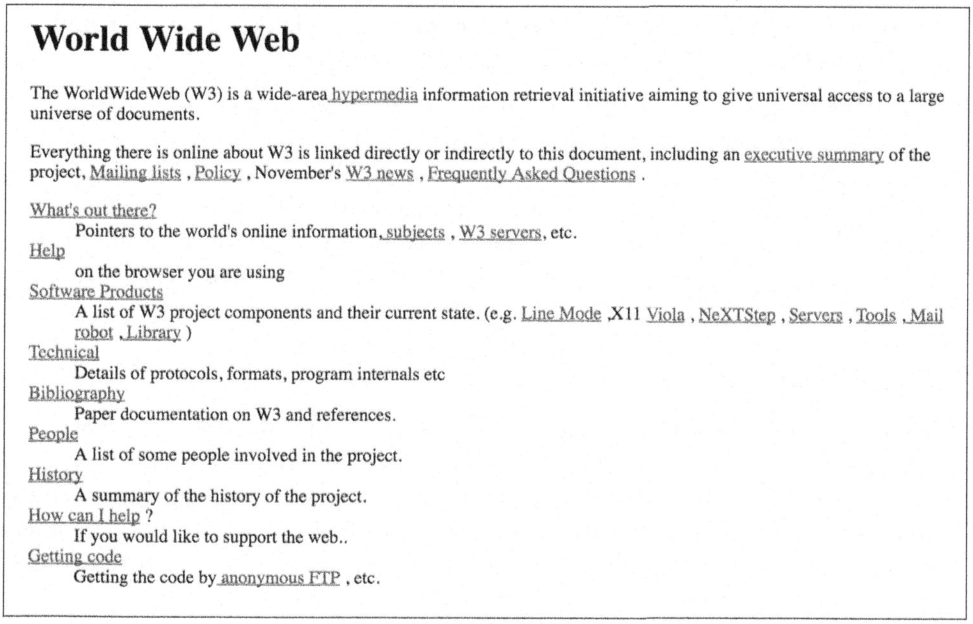

World Wide Web

The WorldWideWeb (W3) is a wide-area hypermedia information retrieval initiative aiming to give universal access to a large universe of documents.

Everything there is online about W3 is linked directly or indirectly to this document, including an executive summary of the project, Mailing lists , Policy , November's W3 news , Frequently Asked Questions .

What's out there?
    Pointers to the world's online information, subjects , W3 servers, etc.
Help
    on the browser you are using
Software Products
    A list of W3 project components and their current state. (e.g. Line Mode ,X11 Viola , NeXTStep , Servers , Tools ,Mail robot ,Library)
Technical
    Details of protocols, formats, program internals etc
Bibliography
    Paper documentation on W3 and references.
People
    A list of some people involved in the project.
History
    A summary of the history of the project.
How can I help ?
    If you would like to support the web..
Getting code
    Getting the code by anonymous FTP , etc.

Figure 1-1. The first website from CERN

Of course, no one called them "static sites" back then as the entire web consisted of static HTML documents—there was no nonstatic alternative.

We've clearly come a long way since then, both in terms of the underlying technologies that make up the web and websites as well as how we expect a website to look and behave. So, why would static sites be a worthwhile option for today's web?

First, let's explore some of the benefits of static sites before we dive into how the changing technology behind static sites (i.e., static site generators—the topic of this book!) are making them viable again.

Benefits of Static Sites

Of the many reasons that static sites are coming back into fashion, two stand out:

- Static sites are fast.
- Static sites are secure.

Static Sites Are Fast

All developers seem to understand that website performance is critical. For example, recent studies (*https://www.soasta.com/blog/google-mobile-web-performance-study/*) have shown that users tend to abandon sites that take longer than three seconds to load (with a load time of under two seconds being considered optimal for mobile). Yet achieving that level of website performance can be difficult.

By their very nature, static sites load extremely fast. This is because every visitor is served the exact same HTML without the bottlenecks caused by a server-side language, database, or any kind of dynamic rendering. Plus, static files are extremely easy to cache and serve via a content delivery network (CDN), making them even faster for the end user. In addition, once you eliminate dynamic rendering from a database, you've eliminated numerous points of failure that often cause sites to be unresponsive or completely fail.

Static Sites Are Secure

Sadly, it is not uncommon nowadays for us to hear about a site being the target of a SQL injection or cross-site scripting (XSS) attack, two of the most common types of website security breaches. Oftentimes, hackers gain access to a site via a vulnerability in the code, many times due to an unpatched CMS. However, with a static site, there is no database to breach and no server-side platform or CMS with unpatched vulnerabilities.

Speaking from personal experience, even a tightly patched and locked-down CMS can be vulnerable. And finding and then repairing the damage done by a breach can be extremely time consuming and difficult.

Obviously, static sites will not eliminate every vulnerability (what will?), but they narrow the window of opportunities available to any hacker and limit the amount of potential damage if a hacker does gain access.

Other Benefits

While those are the two key benefits of static sites, there are certainly others, including:

Flexibility
> You are not working within a CMS framework, so there are no limitations on how you can build your site.

Hosting
> Because there's no need for a database or server-side language support, hosting a static site can be anywhere from inexpensive to completely free, depending on your needs.

Versioning
> Since a static site is made up of static files, it is extremely easy to track and coordinate changes using version control systems like Git and GitHub.

With all these benefits, why wouldn't you choose to use a static site? Well, in truth, only certain kinds of sites can realistically work as static only.

What Kinds of Sites Can Go Static?

There are drawbacks to using static sites. For instance, while some amount of dynamic data is possible on a static site that uses external API calls or third-party services, a static site is simply not suitable if you require a large amount of dynamic data or content personalization. Also, from a development and content contribution standpoint, static site generators (i.e., the tools frequently used to build static sites—and what this book is about) can have a steep learning curve. Lastly, deployment (which we'll talk about in Chapter 7) can be complex, making static sites less than ideal for content that changes frequently.

Keeping those things in mind, sites that tend to work best as static sites are content-focused, infrequently updated (once or twice a day at most, I'd say), and do not require a high degree of user interaction or personalization. Here are some examples of types of sites that work well as static sites:

Blogs
> This is the most common use case; in fact, many static site generators default to a blog template. Blogs are content-focused by design and, in many cases, user interaction is limited to comments, where services like Disqus (*https://disqus.com/*) can fill the requirement.

Documentation

In my experience, this is the second most common use for static sites, because documentation is typically a fixed set of content that tends to update infrequently but which the user expects to get quickly (often on the go). Static sites fit these needs perfectly while providing the potential added benefit of being easy to host on services like GitHub, for versioning and community contribution.

Informational Sites and Brochureware

Much of the web is actually made up of fairly simple websites, such as sites for events, web brochures for small businesses, and community information sites. For these, a CMS would be overkill, but we still want updating to be quick and painless. A static site (using a static site generator) can fit the bill perfectly.

What Are Static Site Generators?

Up to this point, we've mostly been talking about how static sites behave—not how they are built. If we were still in the days of Dreamweaver and—heaven forbid— FrontPage (remember that?), the pain of building and maintaining a static site would outweigh the benefits of having one.

Static site generators solve the pain of building and maintaining a static site. The fundamentals of a static site generator are extremely simple (Figure 1-2): they take in dynamic content, and layout and output static HTML, CSS, and JavaScript files. There are literally hundreds of static site generators (*https://staticsitegenerators.net/*), but essentially they all do exactly the same thing and, for the most part, function similarly.

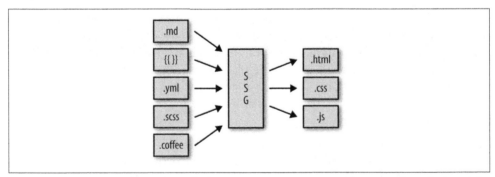

Figure 1-2. A simple illustration of what a static site generator does; it takes a lightweight markup language (e.g., Markdown), a templating language (e.g., Handlebars), and data/ metadata (e.g., Yaml)—and sometimes a CSS preprocessor (e.g., Sass) and a compile-to-JavaScript language (e.g., CoffeeScript)—and generates HTML, CSS, and JavaScript

Most static site generators have the following in common:

- Use one or more templating languages (e.g., Liquid, Handlebars, Jade). This is a key part of any static site generator as it allows you to build a layout/theme for your site and plug in dynamic content during a build.
- Use one or more lightweight markup languages (*http://bit.ly/2lrz8JP*) (e.g., Markdown, AsciiDoc, reStructuredText). Though every static site generator that I've ever tried (and I've tried many) supports straight HTML, using a lightweight markup language makes it quicker and easier to write content using any text editor (provided you've learned the syntax of course).
- Are run via the command line (e.g., terminal or command prompt). Though it is becoming more common for static site generators to include a GUI, most are still designed primarily as a command-line tool.
- Include a local development server. This allows you to develop and test locally before building and deploying your changes. Typically, the tool watches the folder where the site files are being edited and recompiles the site on-the-fly as you edit them.
- Are extensible. In most cases, if your static site generator doesn't support a feature or language that you need, it has a built-in plugin architecture that allows you to add that in (provided you can code in the language the tool is built upon, of course).
- Support file-based data formats (e.g., YAML, TOML, JSON). Lightweight markup languages and HTML are used for long-form content, whereas file-based data allows you to structure any type of data independent of its display.

Additional Background on Static Sites

If you are looking for more details about static sites and how they fit into the larger development ecosystem, I previously published a short report called Static Site Generators: Modern Tools for Static Web Development (O'Reilly, 2015). The report is less focused on technical how-to than this book, and covers the history of static sites, how they differ from dynamic sites built using content management systems or blog engines, and some details about the available static site generators. The report is free and you can download it from O'Reilly here (*http://oreil.ly/2l4fL8j*). Trust me—it's a quick and easy read!

So now that we have a basic understanding of what a static site generator is, how can we use them?

The first issue to resolve is trying to figure out which one to use. This isn't an easy decision since, as of this writing, there are currently 445 different available options (*https://staticsitegenerators.net/*) (Figure 1-3). Even after filtering out projects that haven't been updated recently, we're still left with hundreds of potential tools.

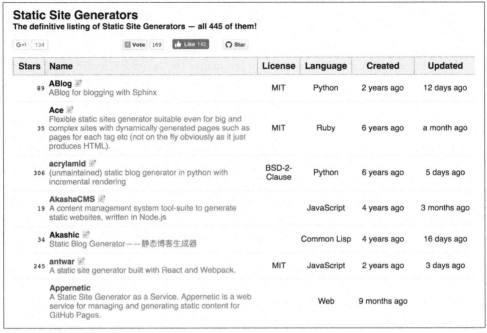

Figure 1-3. StaticSiteGenerators.net (https://staticsitegenerators.net/) is a definitive list of nearly every static site generator project

So how do you choose? I generally recommend that you consider the following factors:

The relative "health" of the project
> How recently has it been updated, and how big and active is the community?

How good is the documentation?
> Unfortunately, many of the hundreds of static site generators (probably a majority) are not well documented. This can cause you to spend far more time than necessary building your site and lead to needless frustration. Review the documentation carefully before committing to a project and don't assume that being able to read the source is sufficient.

Does it support my requirements?
> This can involve very specific requirements (an importer or specific plugin) or a more general ability to meet my needs (is it even extensible?).

Is the language it is built upon important to me?
> For most, a static site generator will work well out of the box. But in some cases, it might be necessary to customize your generator via plugins or even contribu-

tions to the source code. In these special cases, knowing the underlying language can be important.

Over the next few chapters, we'll look at some of the more mature and popular options for developing static sites, including Jekyll, Hugo, and Harp. Not only does each have a different underlying language (Ruby for Jekyll, Go for Hugo, and JavaScript for Harp), which may be an important consideration, but each also has its own pros and cons. We'll look at building some common use cases (a basic informational site, a blog, and a documentation site) using these tools in ways that take advantage of their relative merits. There are obviously other static site generators that could certainly meet all of the above criteria in many circumstances, but, unfortunately, we cannot cover them all.

Once we've built the basics of our static site, we need to add in some dynamic features, like comments on our blog posts or a site search. Or, if we have to support content contributors that aren't comfortable writing posts in Markdown via a text editor, we might want to add a CMS-like backend to our site to allow for easy editing. We'll take a look at multiple solutions that solve each of these problems.

After your static site is complete, it's time to deploy it. While this can be as easy as simply FTPing files onto a server, in most cases you'll want to automate the process or take advantage of services that can manage the build process for you. We'll explore a variety of tools and services that can ease the deployment process.

Finally, you may be evaluating static sites as an option to replace an existing site that uses a tool like WordPress or some other CMS. For these cases, we'll dive into tools that ease the process of migrating to a static site generator from a CMS by bringing over your existing content.

In the end, we hope to provide you with a broad overview of the existing static site generator ecosystem, while diving into the actual implementation details of how to accomplish your goals with these tools.

## CHAPTER 2

Building a Basic Static Site

Raymond Camden

For our first static site, we'll start with something incredibly simple. For some, *brochure-ware* is a derogatory term for a website that looks like it was copied directly from a marketing brochure. While some sites certainly *are* simple copies of marketing material, that doesn't mean there's anything particularly wrong with them.

There are times when a website will be nothing more than one or two pages of content. For example, maybe you're launching the Next Big Thing™ as part of your plan to become a dot-com millionaire. While your product is in development, you may simply need a single-page "Coming Soon" site.

Other examples of simple sites include the following:

- A restaurant site providing hours, address, and a menu
- A landing page for your mobile app that provides links to the various app stores
- A portfolio page that functions as a resume for someone looking for a job

In all of these examples, the entire site might consist of nothing more than one or two unique pages. A static site generator might be overkill for such a thing, but in my experience, small projects have a way of growing—not the other way around. The benefits that static site generators provide will become *more* useful over time as the site (possibly) grows with new content.

For our first example site, we're going to create an online presence for a coffee shop called Camden Grounds. While not a terribly imaginative name, you've probably come across simple coffee-shop/restaurant sites before, so you have a basic idea of how they work. For Camden Grounds, the site will consist of:

- A home page which is mostly pretty images.
- A menu showing a list of various coffees, teas, cookies, and more.

- A list of locations because—wouldn't you know it—Camden Grounds is actually a chain.
- An "About Us" page talking about the history of the company. No one is ever going to read this, but it's pretty standard for such sites.

That's a grand total of four pages and, as I said previously, a static site generator may be a bit much for this, but the good news is that we will be "future-proofed" when we expand the site in the future. For this site, we'll look at our first static site generator in the book, Harp.

Welcome to Harp

Harp (harpjs.com, Figure 2-1) is a lightweight static site generator. It is rather simple and, at times, limited but can be easy to pick up for people new to static sites.

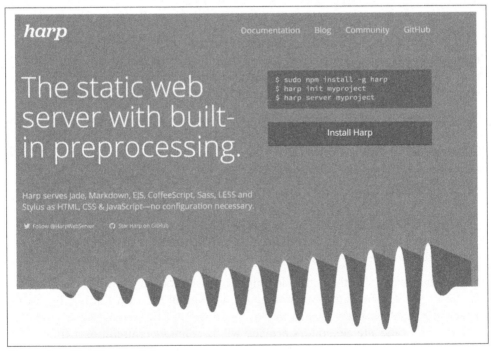

Figure 2-1. The Harp website

Harp requires minimal setup and focuses more on convention than configuration. That's a fancy way of saying that as long as you follow a few simple rules in terms of organization, Harp will "just work." Let's start with installing Harp.

Before you begin, you'll need to ensure that npm is installed on your system. npm stands for Node Package Manager and is commonly used to handle installation for programs. Imagine, for example, that a program requires some other program. Now imagine that program requires something else. The cool thing about npm is that a program developer can define what's required for it to run and the package manager handles the rest. Because of how helpful this is, a great number of utilities use npm. You even already have it installed. The quickest way to find out is to simply go to the terminal if you're using a Mac or the command prompt in Windows and type **npm** (Figure 2-2).

```
● ● ● ▦  working-with-static-site-generators — raymondcamden@Raymonds-MBP — ..te-generators — -zsh...
Last login: Sat Apr  9 10:20:05 on ttys003
[→  working-with-static-site-generators git:(master) ✗ npm

Usage: npm <command>

where <command> is one of:
    access, adduser, bin, bugs, c, cache, completion, config,
    ddp, dedupe, deprecate, dist-tag, docs, edit, explore, faq,
    get, help, help-search, i, init, install, install-test, it,
    link, list, ln, logout, ls, outdated, owner, pack, ping,
    prefix, prune, publish, rb, rebuild, repo, restart, root,
    run-script, s, se, search, set, shrinkwrap, star, stars,
    start, stop, t, tag, team, test, tst, un, uninstall,
    unpublish, unstar, up, update, v, version, view, whoami

npm <cmd> -h     quick help on <cmd>
npm -l           display full usage info
npm faq          commonly asked questions
npm help <term>  search for help on <term>
npm help npm     involved overview

Specify configs in the ini-formatted file:
    /Users/raymondcamden/.npmrc
or on the command line via: npm <command> --key value
Config info can be viewed via: npm help config

npm@3.8.3 /usr/local/lib/node_modules/npm
→  working-with-static-site-generators git:(master) ✗ ▮
```

Figure 2-2. Checking for npm

If this command fails to work, or if you know for sure you don't have npm installed, the easiest way to get it is to install Node.js. Don't worry—you don't have to actually know how to use Node, nor will you ever need to learn it (although Node.js is pretty darn cool and recommended anyway). Head over to nodejs.org (*https://nodejs.org/en/*) and download the installer for your operating system.

Assuming you've got Node installed and npm is working fine, you can install Harp like so:

```
npm install -g harp
```

To confirm Harp installed correctly, simply run harp in your terminal. You should see a nice usage summary, as shown in Figure 2-3.

```
→ working-with-static-site-generators git:(master) x harp

  Usage: harp [options] [command]

  Commands:

    init [options] [path]  Initialize a new Harp project in current directory
    server [options] [path] Start a Harp server in current directory
    multihost [options] [path] Start a Harp server to host a directory of Harp projects
    compile [options] [projectPath] [outputPath] Compile project to static assets (HTML, JS and CSS)

  Options:

    -h, --help     output usage information
    -V, --version  output the version number

  Use 'harp <command> --help' to get more information or visit http://harpjs.com/ to learn more.
```

Figure 2-3. Checking that Harp is installed

Harp has a few different features, but its simplest use is to enable a web server in a directory of files. Instead of just serving up files as they are, Harp supports different preprocessors that enable you to build dynamic resources.

To write HTML:
> You can use Markdown, Jade, or Embedded JavaScript (EJS). By simply using the proper extension (`.md`, `.jade`, or `.ejs`), Harp will automatically convert the syntax for each particular preprocessor into HTML. Of course, if you prefer, you can use regular HTML files instead.

To write CSS:
> You can use Less (`.less`), Sass (`.scss`), or Stylus (`.styl`). Regular CSS files work just fine, too.

To write JavaScript:
> The only option you have is CoffeeScript. Any file with a `.coffee` extension will be converted from CoffeeScript into JavaScript.

You can mix and match any of these preprocessors in any way you see fit. If you don't really care about CSS preprocessing and like JavaScript, then skip those preprocessors and just decide on which HTML preprocessor you want to use. Harp doesn't care.

Your First Harp Project

The Harp CLI supports creating an initial "seed" application, but it may be easier to start more simply. Create an empty folder—it doesn't matter what it's called—and add a file called *index.md*. For our first test, we'll use Markdown, and again, this is completely arbitrary. Example 2-1 shows the contents of the file. You can find this in the GitHub repo (*https://github.com/cfjedimaster/Static-Sites-Book*) of code samples for this book in *code/harp/demo1/index.md*.

Example 2-1. Contents of index.md file

```
Hello World
===

This is a page. Woot.
```

At the command line, ensure that you're in the directory that contains the file, and run `harp server`. You should see Harp start up and describe where it is running, as shown in Figure 2-4.

```
→  demo1 git:(master) ✗ harp server
------------
Harp v0.20.3 - Chloi Inc. 2012–2015
Your server is listening at http://localhost:9000/
Press Ctl+C to stop the server
------------
```

Figure 2-4. Starting the Harp server

If you open your web browser to the address and port shown in your command prompt, you'll see the web page rendered via Harp (Figure 2-5).

Figure 2-5. Harp rendering the Markdown page

Notice how the Markdown was automatically converted into HTML. If you view source or open your browser developer tools, you can see this for yourself (Figure 2-6):

Figure 2-6. The Markdown code has been converted into HTML

Along with converting the Markdown code into HTML, Harp actually makes your file available as an HTML file in the URL as well. If you actually try to access *index.html*, Harp will recognize that *index.md* represents this URL and will serve that file up. This is an important thing to remember. No matter what preprocessor you use, when you actually *link* to pages, or resources, you'll always use the "proper" type for what that preprocessor supports. For example, if you want to add a CSS file and you're using Less, you don't link to `styles.less`, but rather `styles.css` instead.

Learning More About Markdown

If you want to learn more about Markdown, check out its reference guide here: *http://daringfireball.net/projects/markdown/*.

Now let's make another file. *test.jade* will use the Jade template syntax. Here are the contents:

```
h1 This is Jade

a(href="index.html") Go Home
```

In this example, we've used Jade to create a header and a link back to the home page. Notice that we're linking to *index.html*. Again, you do *not* want to link to *index.md* because the final site, when static, will not include those extensions. Figure 2-7 shows the result along with the rendered HTML in Chrome's Dev Tools.

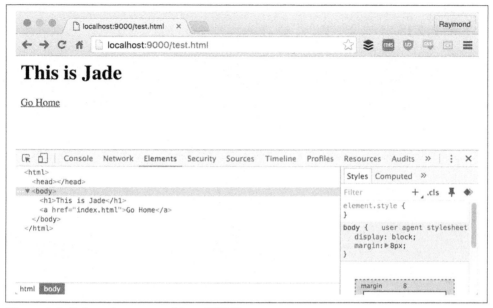

Figure 2-7. Jade code converted into HTML

Learning More About Jade

You can learn more about Jade at its home page: *http://jade-lang.com*.

Finally, let's make another file to demonstrate EJS support. EJS is an older templating language and resembles PHP or Classic ASP in some ways. Unlike Jake and Markdown, which work from almost an abstraction layer over HTML, EJS requires you to write your HTML in—well—TML. You only use EJS's template language when outputting something dynamic. Here's an example of that in action:

```
<h1>This is EJS</h1>

The time is: <%= new Date() %>
```

In this example, the dynamic aspect begins with <%= and ends with >. The inner portion is pure JavaScript and will be executed when the template is rendered. You can find this file in the book repo as *anothertest.ejs* (*http://bit.ly/2m4ARYC*). As before, you can open this in your browser by going to *anothertest.html*, as shown in Figure 2-8. In Figure 2-8, you can see the HTML rendered as is, but notice how the JavaScript was executed.

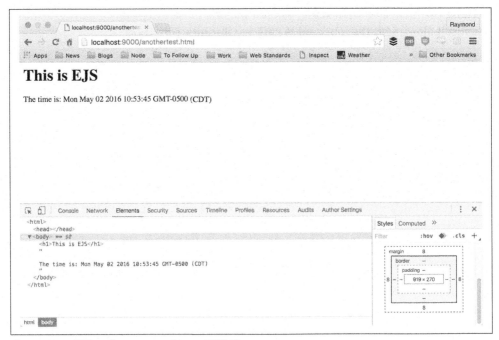

Figure 2-8. EJS code converted into HTML

Learning More About EJS

You can learn more about EJS at its home page: *http://www.embed-dedjs.com/*.

As you can see, there are many different ways to write your HTML. We didn't even touch on the CSS preprocessors. So which do you choose? My suggestion is to play with both and get a feel for which works best for you. The rest of the examples in this chapter will use Jade for consistency's sake.

Working with Layouts and Partials

Now that you've seen how Harp preprocesses templates for you, it's time to kick it up a notch. One of the benefits that a CMS typically provides is the idea of a site-wide layout. For example, you may have a design theme for your site that sets a header, footer, basic colors, etc. The CMS then applies that layout to your content. Moving to static doesn't mean giving up that feature. Harp provides support for layouts by looking for a file named _layout.ext, where ext represents whatever preprocesser you want to use. That means a request for *foo.ejs* will look for *_layout.ejs* or *_layout.jade*.

Yes, you can mix up your layout preprocessor and regular content preprocessor, but that's probably not a good idea.

Harp passes a variable called yield to the layout file that includes the contents of the file requested. Let's see this in action. If you are working with the code from the book repository, you can find the next example in the demo2 folder. We've copied the files from demo1 but also added a new file, _layout.jade:

```
html
    head
        title Harp Site
    body
        != yield
        hr
        p Copyright #{new Date().getFullYear()}
```

This layout isn't terribly exciting, but notice in the middle where we've included the yield variable. This "sucks in" the page that was actually requested and puts it in the layout file. Beneath that, an hr element is used along with a bit of code to include the current year in a copyright notice.

Now when you request one of the previous files, you'll see it wrapped in the layout, as you can see in Figure 2-9.

Figure 2-9. Layout applied to pages

By default, Harp will look in the current folder before it looks in folders higher in the project directory. This means you can create a customized layout for a subdirectory. Later on when we look at how to work with data, you'll see another way to modify layout as well.

Partials are simply a way for one template to include another. Imagine you have a bit of boilerplate legal text, such as the typical license agreement text that no one actually reads. If you need that text in a few different pages, Harp provides a simple way to include that text in your templates. Let's look at an example.

```
h1 This is Jade

!= partial("_legal")

a(href="index.html") Go Home
```

In the Jade template above, the `partial` function is passed `_legal` as an argument. This tells Harp to look for a file named *_legal.ext* where the extension can be *.jade, .ejs, .md*. The extension is *not* included in the call.

Here's a version in EJS:

```
<h1>This is EJS</h1>

<%- partial("_legal") %>

The time is: <%= new Date() %>
```

Same basic concept as the Jade version—you tell Harp the name of the file minus the extension. Unfortunately, you can't use the `partial` function within a Markdown file. You can include a Markdown file, but a Markdown file itself can't include items. As for what you put in the included file, it can be whatever you want.

Here is a Jade template that simply outputs a tiny bit of legalese:

```
pre This is some boring legal text.
```

In Figure 2-10, you can see both the Jade and EJS templates with the same file.

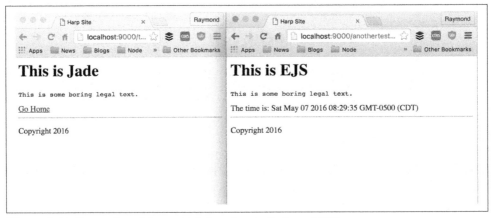

Figure 2-10. Examples of the partial function in Jade and EJS

Partials can be made even more powerful by passing variables to them. This covers the use case where you want to include common code in templates but slightly tweak them every now and then. To pass a variable to an include loaded via `partial`, you simply include a second argument in your call.

Here is an example:

```
h1 Testing Variables

!= partial("_greeting", {name:"Raymond"})
```

In this Jade example (and of course you can do this in EJS as well), the second argument is a plain JavaScript object of name/value pairs. In this case, we have one value for `name`. You can have as many name/value pairs as you would like. On the partial side, you display the variable as you see fit. Here's `_greeting.jade`:

```
h3 Hello #{name}
```

Obviously, this will display "Hello Raymond", and if you change the variable, then the output will change as well.

All of the previous demos for the `partial` function may be found in the `demo3` folder. As a final note, you may wonder why the partials we used were named with an underscore in front. That is *not* a requirement. However, Harp has a feature where any filename beginning with an underscore will not be converted to a static file. For partials, it makes sense that we don't need them generated as is, so using an underscore in front of the name ensures we won't end up with stray static files we don't need.

Working with Data

So far, we've seen how Harp can convert multiple types of templates into simple HTML pages (and don't forget that Harp also supports this for CSS and JavaScript) as well as how to use layouts and partials. Now let's kick it up a notch and talk about how you can add data to a project to use within templates. Generally, data in Harp comes in two forms: global data and metadata. Global data is useful for things that apply to the site as a whole. For example, you may want to store a contact email address in data so you can easily change it one place. Conversely, metadata is more useful for describing specific parts of your site. For example, given that you have a blog, you can use metadata to describe your blog entries (e.g., their titles and publication dates). Let's start with global data.

In your Harp project, you can add a file named `_harp.json`. The contents should be valid JSON and contain a top-level "key" called `globals`. Inside of this should be a set of name/value pairs for whatever data you want to use in your site.

Here is an example:

```
{
        "globals":{
                "title":"My Site!",
                "owner":"Raymond Camden"
        }
}
```

In this example, we have two values—one for `title` and one for `owner`. To be clear, this is *completely arbitrary*. You can use whatever makes sense for you here. Your values also need not be simple strings. As long as it is valid JSON, you can use whatever you want, including arrays.

```
{
    "globals":{
        "title":"My Site!",
        "owner":"Raymond Camden",
        "subjects":["Math","Science","Beer"]
    }
}
```

Once defined, you can use these variables in any of your templates, whether it be a regular template, layout file, or partial. How you use it depends on the language. For Jade, it would look like this:

```
p #{ owner }
```

In EJS, it would look like so:

```
<p><%= owner %></p>
```

Let's look at an example of this in action. In the `demo4` folder, you'll find a complete example that includes a home page, a layout, and a *_harp.json* file. The contents of the globals match the previous code example so we won't share it again. Here's the home page.

```
h1 This is my site.

p Welcome to my site. Sorry this isn't more exciting.

p This site was made by #{owner}.
```

The `owner` value from *_harp.json* is used within a simple paragraph tag. Now let's look at the layout.

```
html
    head
        title #{title}
    body
        != yield
        hr
        p Copyright #{new Date().getFullYear()}
```

In this version, the layout is now dynamic based on the global variable. Note that we still have a dynamic copyright as well. You can mix and match global variables with things defined locally on the template. We could replace that code with a global variable, but then we'd have to edit the year every New Year's Eve and no one wants to do that.

View it in your browser to see it in action (Figure 2-11). Simply change the values, reload the page, and you can see your change reflected immediately.

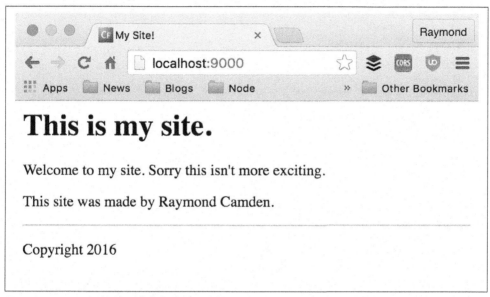

Figure 2-11. Examples of global variables

Now let's consider metadata. This can be a slightly confusing topic so let's start off with an example. Imagine you're building a simple store. Your website will consist of a home page and a product page for each of your products. The folder, *demo5*, will be the basis for this site. Figure 2-12 shows that it has a home page, a layout, and a folder of products.

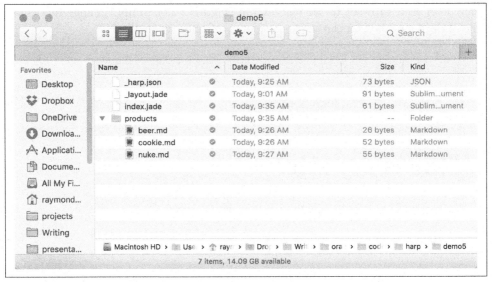

Figure 2-12. Version one of the product site

If you run this with `harp server`, you can request the home page and then each individual product page. If you wanted to link to the products from the home page, how would you do it?

Since you only have three products, you could just hard code a simple list. That certainly works, but isn't really scalable. What if you had a hundred products? What if you wanted your home page to only list the most recently released products and keep a complete list of products on some other page? This is where metadata comes into play.

To begin, create a new file in your *products* folder called *_data.json*. As with the globals file, it must be a valid JSON file. In this file, describe your data. Let's consider the following example.

```
{
        "nuke": {
                "title":"A Nuke",
                "price":9.99
        },
        "cookie":{
                "title":"Cookies",
                "price":2.99
        },
        "beer":{
                "title":"Beer",
                "price":8.99
        }
}
```

In this JSON file, we have three main parts—one for each product. The names—nuke, cookie, and beer—match the filenames from the demo. This will become important in a moment. Inside each block of data are two variables—title and price. As before, this is arbitrary. But here's where things get interesting.

The first change is that Harp will now recognize this data and make it available to your templates. Any template can access this data via a new variable, public.prod ucts._data. The public variable is always available in Harp projects. The products key comes from the fact that we have a folder called products. Finally, _data maps to the _data.json_ file itself. What this means then is that we can create a dynamic list of products. Here's an updated home page that now creates a list of links.

```
h1 Welcome to our store

ul
  for product, link in public.products._data
    li
      a(href='/products/#{link}.html') #{product.title} ($#{product.price})

p This site was made by #{owner}.
```

Let's break this down. The for loop iterates over the data, grabbing two values. prod uct represents the individual product. Notice how we include the title and price. The link variable is the top-level key in the JSON file, namely "nuke", "cookie", and "beer". Remember how we said we made it match the filenames? That then lets us create links to the product files. Because we have access to the raw data, we could even do something complex, such as re-sorting the values by price or title. Figure 2-13 shows a screenshot of the home page now including the links.

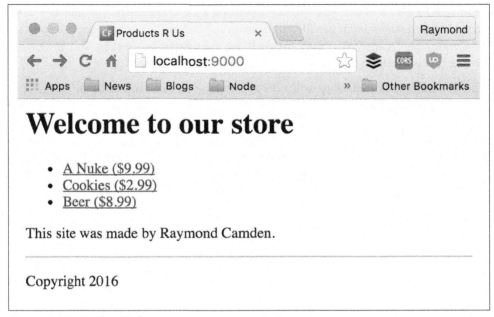

Figure 2-13. Product links

Now you can click on the links and go directly to each product page. But here's where things get even more interesting. Consider the beer page shown in Figure 2-14.

Figure 2-14. The beer page

Notice anything in particular? See how the title changed? What happened there? When Harp works with variables, it does something special with metadata. Harp recognized that *beer.md* was being loaded, and that "beer" matched the value in *_data.json*. Because of this match, when Harp checks variables, it will look in _data.json_ before it checks globals defined in _harp.json_. This allows you to dynamically update values on a page-by-page basis. It's perfect for cases where you may want a default, global title for a site but have specific titles for each product.

Generating a Site

Now that you've seen the basics of how to use Harp and work with dynamic templates, how do you actually create static output? The basic command with the CLI is: `harp compile pathToCode pathToOutput`. A full example could look like this: `harp compile ./ ../output`. This tells Harp to compile the current directory and output the result in a folder above the current path named `output`. Given the input from the last demo (`demo6`), the output looks like Figure 2-15:

Name	^	Date Modified
index.html	⊘	Today, 11:10 AM
▼ 📁 products	⊘	Today, 11:10 AM
beer.html	⊘	Today, 11:10 AM
cookie.html	⊘	Today, 11:10 AM
nuke.html	⊘	Today, 11:10 AM

Figure 2-15. Compiled output

Notice how the _.jade_ and _.md_ files are now all regular HTML files. Also, all the "special" files (layout- and data-related) are gone.

Building Camden Grounds

We began this chapter by explaining what we would build as an example of a fairly simple site—a coffee shop named Camden Grounds. We described this as a site with four pages—a home page, menu, list of locations, and a simple "About Us" that frankly no one will ever read. (But don't tell the client that!)

To create this site, we first need a design. If you're like me (with little to no design skill), you'll probably want to either hire a designer or find a website template that you can use. Luckily, the website freewebsitetemplates.com actually has one called "Coffee Shop Web Template" (_http://bit.ly/2miA428_) that is both perfect and free.

As a word of caution, before deciding to use any template, it is a good idea to take a look at the source code behind it. It could be an incredibly good-looking web page with an absolutely horrible mess of code behind it. In this case, the shop template was fairly simple and easy to work with. Figure 2-16 shows the template in its original form:

Figure 2-16. Original coffee shop web template

It matches perfectly with our requirements except for the Blog item. Luckily, we can just remove it. You can find the complete source code for this demo in the *ch2/camdengrounds* (*http://bit.ly/2kIpMMm*) folder, but let's go over the files one by one so you can see how it is put together.

First, let's look at the template. This was created by looking at a few of the files from the template and determining which content remained the same. As you can imagine, this is the header and footer. Since a majority of the template is regular HTML, Example 2-2 focuses on the dynamic, more interesting aspects of the template. See the original file (*_layout.ejs*) for the complete listing.

Example 2-2. Dynamic aspects of the coffee shop web template

```
<div id="header">
  <a href="/index.html">
  <img src="/images/logo.png" alt="Image">
  </a>
  <ul>
    <li
      <% if(current.source == 'index') { %>
      class="current"
      <% } %>
      >

      <a href="/index.html">Home</a>
    </li>
    <li
      <% if(current.source == 'menu') { %>
      class="current"
      <% } %>
      >
      <a href="/menu.html">Menu</a>
    </li>
    <li
      <% if(current.source == 'locations') { %>
      class="current"
      <% } %>
      >
      <a href="/locations.html">Locations</a>
    </li>
    <li
      <% if(current.source == 'about') { %>
      class="current"
      <% } %>
      >
      <a href="/about.html">About Us</a>
    </li>
  </ul>
</div>
<div id="body">
<%- yield %>
</div>
```

The first thing to make note of is in the header menu; note the use of a variable called
current:

```
<li
        <% if(current.source == 'index') { %>
        class="current"
        <% } %>
        >
                <a href="/index.html">Home</a>
</li>
```

The `current` object is a helper value that Harp provides to each template. It has two values: `source` and `path`. The `path` value represents the current "directory hierarchy" of the request. So given a request like raymondcamden.com/products/weapons/ foo.html, the `path` value would be an array consisting of: `products`, `weapons`, `foo`. The `source` value is just the very end of the hierarchy, so given the same URL, you would get a value of foo. As you can imagine, this is a useful way of saying, "I'm on page so and so, do so and so." The code snippet above basically handles adding a CSS class to each menu item when the user is on a particular page. Similar code is used in the bottom menu. Finally, don't forget that your layout file has to include the `yield` variable to display the contents of the template.

Let's now look at the pages. It will be easier to start with the simplest page, *about.html*, as it is just simple text. Remember that we don't have to include the layout. Example 2-3 shows *about.ejs* with some of the boilerplate text removed to save space:

Example 2-3. Simple text of the about.html page

```
<div id="figure">
        <img src="images/headline-about.jpg" alt="Image">
        <span>Lorem ipsum dolor sit amet.</span>
</div>
<div>
  <a href="about.html" class="about">About</a>
  <div>

      <h3>We Have Coffee for Everyone</h3>
      <p>
      Mauris sed libero ac neque lobortis aliquam. Vivamus vitae ultricies.
        </p>

      <h3>We Even Have Tea!</h3>
      <p>
      Sed a pretium risus, ut volutpat nunc. Donec blandit orci id sollicitn.
      </p>

      <h3>We Don't Have Beer</h3>
      <p>
      Proin dapibus, orci vitae bibendum laoreet, libero velit condimentum
      </p>
```

```
    </div>
</div>
```

There's nothing dynamic here, so the only real content is the text describing the company. Figure 2-17 shows it as run under Harp—notice how the menu recognizes what page is being displayed.

Figure 2-17. About Us page

Now let's move to the Locations page. This one will be a bit tricky. Though there aren't many locations now, Camden Grounds hopes to grow into a mega-coffee-serving chain to rival that of a certain company out of Seattle. The locations page therefore should be dynamic to make it easy to add locations later on. Let's first look at a screenshot (shown in Figure 2-18), and then we'll explain how it was built.

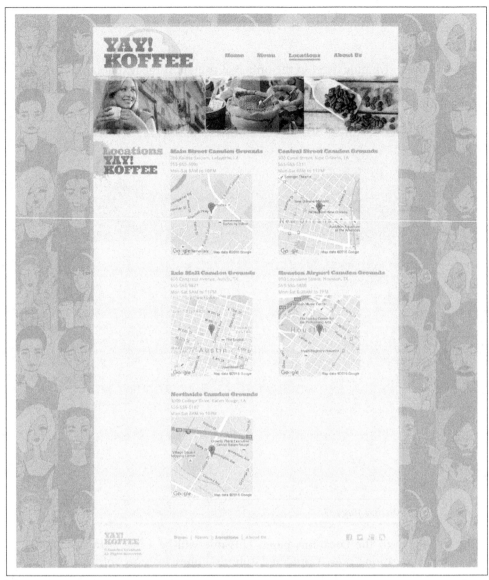

Figure 2-18. Locations page

Each location is rendered as a name, an address, phone numbers, hours of operation, and a little map. How is this done? First, we added location data to the *_harp.json* file as a global. Example 2-4 shows that file, with a few locations removed for brevity.

Example 2-4. _harp.json file of the locations page

```json
{
    "globals":{
        "locations":[
            {
                "name":"Main Street Camden Grounds",
                "address":"200 Kaliste Saloom, Lafayette, LA",
                "hours":"Mon-Sat 6AM to 10PM",
                "phone":"555-555-5001"
            },
            {
                "name":"Northside Camden Grounds",
                "address":"3009 College Drive, Baton Rouge, LA",
                "hours":"Mon-Sat 6AM to 10PM",
                "phone":"555-555-5107"
            }
        ]
    }
}
```

Now let's look at the template code, shown here in Example 2-5.

Example 2-5. Template code for locations page

```html
<div id="figure">
    <img src="images/headline-locations.jpg" alt="Image">
</div>
<div>
    <a href="locations.html" class="locations">Locations</a>
    <div>
        <% for(idx in locations) { %>
        <dl>
            <dt><%- locations[idx].name %></dt>
            <dd><%- locations[idx].address %></dd>
            <dd><%- locations[idx].phone %></dd>
            <dd><%- locations[idx].hours %></dd>
            <dd>
                <img
src="https://maps.googleapis.com/maps/api/staticmap?center=
<%- locations[idx].address %>
&size=250x250&zoom=15&markers=color:red%7Clabel:S%7C
<%- locations[idx].address %>
&key=AIzaSyB3eiEtldYqoxbVyN5wq_-PqvV7xrDuUQA">
            </dd>
        </dl>
        <% } %>
    </div>
</div>
```

The list of locations is iterated as a JavaScript array. Each item is output per the original template design but with some modifications to fit our data. Finally, the Google Static Maps API (a very handy Google service that doesn't get a lot of attention) is used to display a small map of the location. Note that Google requires you to get a key to use this service. There is a free tier that is more than appropriate for simple static sites.

Fairly simple—but the big win here is that when Camden Grounds expands, all you need to do is edit the pure data to have the site updated. (And, of course, generate the static version and deploy it.)

Now it's time to kick it up a notch. Handling the menu for Camden Grounds will be a two-step process. First, we will make a unique page for each menu item. We'll store that under a *coffees* directory. Each page will include text about the product, but for now we've kept it down to just one simple sentence. As before, let's look at a menu page and then we'll cover how it was built. Here is *coffee1.ejs*:

```
<%- partial("_coffee_header") %>

<p>
This is coffee 1.
</p>

<%- partial("_coffee_footer") %>
```

Obviously, this would be a bit longer for a real product, but you can see in Example 2-6 where we're using partials to include header and footer layout for the item. (As an aside, you can do nested layouts in Harp, but it is somewhat complex.) The footer is just a few closing div tags, but the header is a bit dynamic:

Example 2-6. Partials to include headers and footers

```
<div id="figure">
        <img src="/images/headline-menu.jpg" alt="Image">
        <span><%- name %></span>
</div>

<div>
        <a href="/menu.html" class="whatshot">What&#39;s Hot</a>
        <div>

<img src="/images/<%- image %>" alt="<%- name %>" style="float:right">
```

What's going on here? We're outputting a name and image, but where does this come from? Well, remember that we can supply metadata for our content. Let's now take a look at that in Example 2-7. (As with other code listings, we've trimmed it a bit.)

Example 2-7. Supplying metadata for our content

```
{
        "coffee1":{
                "name":"Coffee One",
                "price":2.99,
                "image":"coffee1.jpg",
                "short":"Creamy"
        },
        "coffee2":{
                "name":"Coffee Two",
                "price":9.99,
                "image":"coffee2.jpg",
                "short":"Rich"
        },
        "coffee6":{
                "name":"Coffee Six",
                "price":4.99,
                "image":"coffee6.jpg",
                "short":"Weird"
        }
}
```

Each menu item has a key that matches with its filename, and then some basic information about the menu item. Notice that we aren't using all of that data. You'll see where we actually do in a moment. Figure 2-19 is the page for the first coffee.

Figure 2-19. Menu item page

So what about the menu itself? Since we've created a few products and have metadata defined in *_data.json*, we can make use of it to render a dynamic menu. Example 2-8 shows how we do that.

Example 2-8. Rendering a dynamic menu

```
<ul>
<% for(idx in public.coffees._data) { %>
      <li>
            <a href="/coffees/<%- idx %>.html">
            <img src="images/<%- public.coffees._data[idx].image %>"
            alt="<%- public.coffees._data[idx].name %>"></a>
            <div>
                  <a href="/coffees/<%- idx %>.html">
                  <%- public.coffees._data[idx].name %></a>
                  <p>
                        <%- public.coffees._data[idx].short %>
                        &#36;<%- public.coffees._data[idx].price %>
                  </p>
            </div>
      </li>
```

```
<% } %>
</ul>
```

Remember that Harp places metadata in a `public.X` object where X represents the folder containing the data file. This lets us loop over each menu item and list out the name, short description, price, and image. Figure 2-20 shows the menu.

Figure 2-20. Menu page

We're almost done. The final page is the home page. This is somewhat modified from the original template as we don't have a blog anymore. Instead, we're going to display three products. In theory, we could sort these by the most expensive or best selling, but for now we'll just grab the first three. Example 2-9 shows the code.

Example 2-9. Home page code displaying products

```
<div id="figure">
        <img src="images/headline-home.jpg" alt="Image">
        <span id="home">Camden Grounds is the best darn coffee in the world!
        <a href="about.html">Find out why.</a></span>
</div>
<div id="featured">
        <span class="whatshot"><a href="menu.html">Find out more</a></span>
        <div>
                <%
                        coffeeKeys = Object.keys(public.coffees._data);
                        for(var x = 0; x<Math.min(coffeeKeys.length,3);x++) {
                                coffee = public.coffees._data[coffeeKeys[x]];
                %>
                                <a href="/coffees/<%- coffeeKeys[x] %>.html">
                                <img src="images/<%- coffee.image %>"
                                alt="<%- coffee.name %>"></a>
                <% } %>
        </div>
</div>
```

In general, this isn't too different from the menu page, but instead we grab the keys from the data and loop until we hit either the total number of items or 3. The result is pretty much as you expect and is shown in Figure 2-21.

Figure 2-21. Home Page

Obviously, there's more that could be done, but we hope you can see how Harp really makes it easy to manage this simple little website.

Going Further with Harp

As we said in the beginning, we were only going to scratch the surface of the Harp static site generator. Here is a quick look at some of the features we did not cover in this chapter:

- While we documented it, we didn't show any CSS or JavaScript preprocessing. Don't forget that Harp allows for this as well.
- Harp provides access to a `_contents` variable that represents each folder in the project. This could be useful for generating a dynamic list of images for an art gallery.
- Harp sets an `environment` variable that represents development versus production. This lets you toggle certain things based on where your code is running.
- Harp provides basic 404 and client-side routing support.
- Harp can be used inside another Node.js application.

For more information, see the Harp documentation (*http://harpjs.com/docs/*).

## CHAPTER 3

Building a Blog

Raymond Camden

Blogs are one of the most popular type of sites on the internet. In fact, WordPress, an open source blogging engine, is currently used by over 60 million bloggers.

At its heart, a blog is fairly simple. Like a diary, each entry in the blog is an individual story and typically presented to the user in reverse chronological order. Blogs will also usually have categories to organize entries. Visitors can then read more entries in a particular category to focus on things that may interest them more.

In this chapter, we're going to build a simple blog. The static site generator we'll be using in this chapter actually builds a blog out of the box, so not much time will be spent on building a *specific* blog per se. But we will demonstrate how to find a real blog template, implement it, and then create some temporary content so we can see the blog in action.

Last-Minute Change

Jekyll released a major update right before the publication of this book. While basic operations are the same, some screenshots may look slightly different on your installation. Any serious issues will be reported in the book's errata.

Blogging with Jekyll

Jekyll (*https://jekyllrb.com*) is a static site generator focused on creating blogs (Figure 3-1). While it certainly can be used to build non-blog sites, out of the box its primary use is creating blogs. It also integrates natively with GitHub Pages, which provides you a free hosting option for your site as well. (Since the site has to run on a

GitHub project itself, naturally the blog then has to be *about* the project itself, although GitHub also lets you run one personal site for your account as a whole.)

Figure 3-1. The Jekyll website

Installation of Jekyll is a bit more complex than other static site generators. Right away, be aware that Jekyll is *not* officially supported on Windows. You can find documentation for "making it work" on Windows, and that should be good enough to follow along with this chapter, but if your primary OS is Windows, you may want to triple-check how well it works before committing to Jekyll.

Before installing Jekyll, you need to install Ruby (*https://www.ruby-lang.org/en/down loads/*) and RubyGems (*https://rubygems.org/pages/download*). You won't need to know anything about Ruby to use Jekyll (although it helps when building custom plugins), so don't worry if you've never worked with the programming language before.

Once you have RubyGems installed, you can use the command line to install Jekyll:

```
gem install jekyll
```

Once installed, open up your terminal and type **jekyll** to ensure it's been installed correctly. Figure 3-2 shows what you should see.

```
→ working-with-static-site-generators git:(master) ✗ jekyll
A subcommand is required.
jekyll 3.1.3 -- Jekyll is a blog-aware, static site generator in Ruby

Usage:

  jekyll <subcommand> [options]

Options:
        -s, --source [DIR]  Source directory (defaults to ./)
        -d, --destination [DIR]  Destination directory (defaults to ./_site)
            --safe          Safe mode (defaults to false)
        -p, --plugins PLUGINS_DIR1[,PLUGINS_DIR2[,...]]  Plugins directory (defaults to ./_plugins)
            --layouts DIR   Layouts directory (defaults to ./_layouts)
            --profile       Generate a Liquid rendering profile
        -h, --help          Show this message
        -v, --version       Print the name and version
        -t, --trace         Show the full backtrace when an error occurs

Subcommands:
  docs
  build, b               Build your site
  clean                  Clean the site (removes site output and metadata file) without building.
  doctor, hyde           Search site and print specific deprecation warnings
  help                   Show the help message, optionally for a given subcommand.
  new                    Creates a new Jekyll site scaffold in PATH
  serve, server, s       Serve your site locally
  import                 Import your old blog to Jekyll
```

Figure 3-2. Testing for Jekyll at the prompt

Jekyll supports creating content in either regular HTML or Markdown files. HTML files are served as is, but Markdown files will be converted to HTML first. On top of this, it supports a template language called Liquid (*https://github.com/Shopify/liquid/wiki*). Liquid is incredibly powerful and you'll see multiple examples of that in this chapter, but it integrates well with your existing HTML. This is where you'll create dynamic content locally that ends up being static when done. Adding another layer to the mix is front matter. *Front matter* is metadata on top of the page that tells Jekyll how to parse the page. All of this will make a lot more sense once you see a few examples.

Plugins

You can also use plugins with Jekyll to add support for other templating languages.

Your First Jekyll Project

Now that you have Jekyll installed, it is time to create your first site. Out of the box, Jekyll creates a "complete" but mostly empty blog. You'll have a layout, a home page showing your blog posts, and one written post. Creating a new Jekyll site is as easy as typing **jekyll new foo**, where foo represents the path to the new site (Figure 3-3).

```
→ ch3 git:(master) ✗ jekyll new demo1
New jekyll site installed in /Users/raymondcamden/Dropbox/Writing/ora static sites/ch3/demo1.
→ ch3 git:(master) ✗ ▊
```

Figure 3-3. Creating a new Jekyll site

Jekyll will install various dependencies necessary for the site and default theme, and then complete the installation. Next, change directories into the new directory the CLI created and start the server by running `jekyll serve`, as shown in Figure 3-4. (Jekyll provides a few alternatives to that command as well, like `jekyll s`.)

```
→ demo1 git:(master) ✗ jekyll serve
Configuration file: /Users/raymondcamden/Dropbox/Writing/ora static sites/ch3/demo1/_config.yml
           Source: /Users/raymondcamden/Dropbox/Writing/ora static sites/ch3/demo1
      Destination: /Users/raymondcamden/Dropbox/Writing/ora static sites/ch3/demo1/_site
 Incremental build: disabled. Enable with --incremental
       Generating...
                    done in 0.48 seconds.
 Auto-regeneration: enabled for '/Users/raymondcamden/Dropbox/Writing/ora static sites/ch3/demo1'
Configuration file: /Users/raymondcamden/Dropbox/Writing/ora static sites/ch3/demo1/_config.yml
    Server address: http://127.0.0.1:4000/
  Server running... press ctrl-c to stop.
▊
```

Figure 3-4. Starting up the Jekyll server

You can now open up your browser to the address reported by the command line and you'll see something like Figure 3-5.

Figure 3-5. The default site created by Jekyll

There are a few things to note here. First off, the simplistic UI you see is just a default. It is absolutely *not* something you have to use. Later in the chapter, you'll see an example that has its own custom UI. You also have two content examples. The About link on top shows a simple page, while the Welcome to Jekyll! link shows a sample blog post, as shown in Figure 3-6. You should definitely click that link because the page provides some good explanatory text along with a sample of how code snippets are rendered.

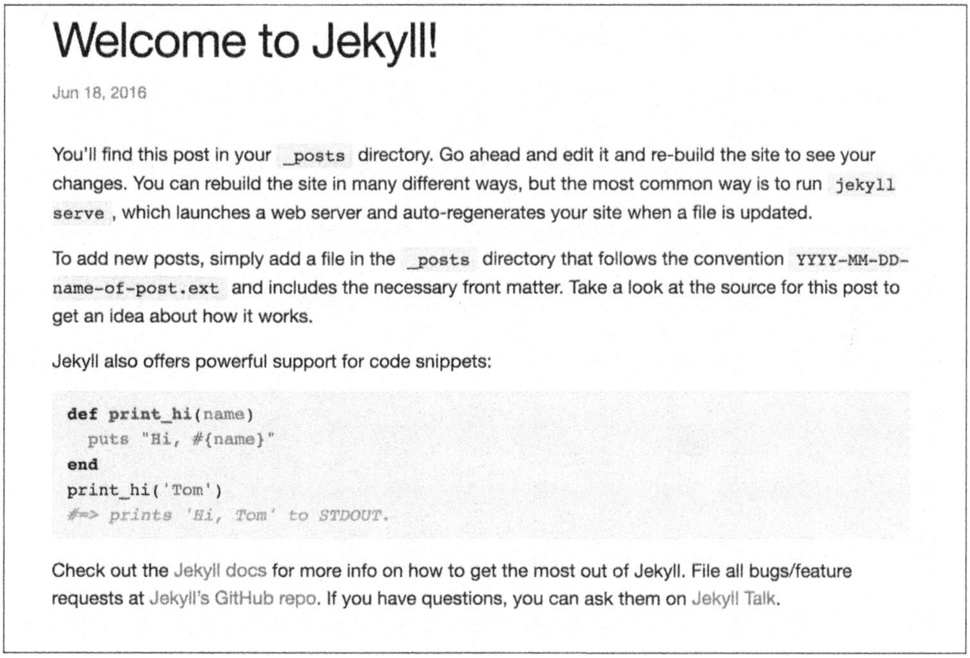

Welcome to Jekyll!

Jun 18, 2016

You'll find this post in your `_posts` directory. Go ahead and edit it and re-build the site to see your changes. You can rebuild the site in many different ways, but the most common way is to run `jekyll serve`, which launches a web server and auto-regenerates your site when a file is updated.

To add new posts, simply add a file in the `_posts` directory that follows the convention `YYYY-MM-DD-name-of-post.ext` and includes the necessary front matter. Take a look at the source for this post to get an idea about how it works.

Jekyll also offers powerful support for code snippets:

```ruby
def print_hi(name)
  puts "Hi, #{name}"
end
print_hi('Tom')
#=> prints 'Hi, Tom' to STDOUT.
```

Check out the Jekyll docs for more info on how to get the most out of Jekyll. File all bugs/feature requests at Jekyll's GitHub repo. If you have questions, you can ask them on Jekyll Talk.

Figure 3-6. A sample post from the Jekyll server

Now let's take a look at the directory structure of your Jekyll project.

Another Last-Minute Change

The very latest version of Jekyll uses a theme that runs from a special directory on your machine used by RubyGems. This means you will *not* see the theme files in your site. This is a cool change in that it keeps themes in one central location, but on the other hand, it makes it a bit difficult to play around and tweak a theme to your liking. In order to correct this, you can ask for the location of the theme by doing this:

```
bundle show minima
```

minima is the name of the theme. This will return a path like this:

```
/Library/Ruby/Gems/2.0.0/gems/minima-2.1.0
```

Given that you're in the directory of the Jekyll site you just created, you can copy the files like so:

```
cp -r /Library/Ruby/Gems/2.0.0/gems/minima-2.1.0/ .
```

Note that the examples provided in the book's GitHub repository (*https://github.com/cfjedimaster/Static-Sites-Book*) already have their theme files in place (Figure 3-7).

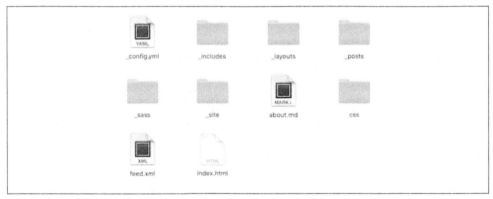

Figure 3-7. Folders and files created by Jekyll

Let's discuss these files and folders left to right, top to bottom:

_config.yml
> This is a configuration file that helps drive how Jekyll operates. You can provide configuration values here as well as in the command line, but it is easier to set things in the file so you don't have to repeat yourself at the command prompt.

_includes
> This is a folder specifically for items you will include in your templates. For example, a boilerplate legal agreement used in multiple locations throughout your site could be written as an include. Jekyll refers to these files as *partials*.

`_layouts`
> This is where you put files that handle the layout of your site. You may have one layout or multiple. Jekyll supports creating as many as you like.

`_posts`
> This is where you create new files for blog content.

`_sass`
> This is for Sass CSS files. They will automatically be converted into CSS by Jekyll and copied to the `css` folder when creating your static site. Using Sass is optional and you can skip this if you want to write plain CSS.

`_site`
> This is the static version of your site. This is created as you work. In a brand-new created project, this folder may not exist yet, but will be made as soon as you run the Jekyll server or specifically use the CLI to generate static output.

about.md and index.html
> These are files created by Jekyll by default. They represent a simple About page and a home page. You can remove any of these (although you should keep a home page) and add whatever makes sense. For example, if you want a Contact page, you could add it here. Note that using Markdown is optional, and you can pick and choose which files you want to use Markdown with, as the default files demonstrate.

Any other folders created that Jekyll doesn't recognize or work with
> These will be copied as is into your static site. For example, if you added a `js` folder for your JavaScripts, these would be copied as is. The exception to this is folders preceded by underscores. These will be ignored, and thus could be used for site assets you don't want copied to the output.

Additional Folders

There are more folders that Jekyll will automatically recognize, and you'll see examples of them later in the book.

Writing a Post

Now that we've got a blog up and running, let's create a new post. When you write a new post, Jekyll expects you to follow a particular naming scheme for the file. The format is: `YEAR-MONTH-DAY-title.extension`. Create a new file called *2016-06-25-new-post.html*. By using *html* as the extension, we're specifically saying we don't want to use Markdown. Feel free to use `md` (or `markdown`) if you want. Also feel free to change the date values to the current date.

Every post you write must begin with *front matter*, which is simply metadata about the post that lives on top of the page in a format called *YAML*. It may help to take a look at the YAML in the existing page created by Jekyll, shown in Example 3-1. (Note that your YAML may be slightly different depending on the date you created the demo.)

Example 3-1. YAML format in Jekyll

```
---
layout: post
title:  "Welcome to Jekyll!"
date:   2016-06-18 09:18:33 -0500
categories: jekyll update
---
```

YAML formats data in a simple key/value system. You can see four keys and four values in Example 3-1. You can get more complex if you need to. The Wikipedia YAML page (*https://en.wikipedia.org/wiki/YAML*) is a good resource for learning more about the YAML format, but you won't (typically) need to get too complex in your Jekyll files.

Dates in Front Matter and Filesystem

You may have noticed that both the filename itself and the front matter include date information. The date in the front matter will take precedence over the filename. If you don't need to specify a time and you're happy with the date in the filename, simply remove the date from the front matter.

Go ahead and open the new file and create the front matter and content:

```
---
layout: post
title:  "Hello World!"
date:   2016-06-25 09:51:33 -0500
categories: general
---

<p>
This is a test!
</p>
```

The first item, `layout`, tells Jekyll what layout file to use for rendering content. We'll look at layouts in the next section. The `title` value is—obviously—what will be the title for the post. The `date` value represents when you created the content. You can specify any value you want here, but if you specify a time in the future, Jekyll will assume this is content for publication at a later time. (You can tell Jekyll to display posts in the future by using `--future` at the command line or by editing your configuration file.)

The final value, `categories`, represents the categories this blog entry should go in. These categories are completely arbitrary. You can look at the values used in the initial post as an example, and going forward, pick ones that make sense for your site. So if you're creating a pet blog, categories could include dog, cat, and dragon. Finally, the actual content of the post is just one paragraph. Save the file, and then reload your Jekyll blog. As you can see in Figure 3-8, Jekyll automatically includes the post.

Posts

Jun 25, 2016
Hello World!

Jun 18, 2016
Welcome to Jekyll!

subscribe via RSS

Figure 3-8. Your new post shows up automatically

Notice how it appears above the previous post; that's because you used a date that follows the initial post. If you modify the date and set an earlier value for the year, it will automatically move down below the first post. Click the link and you'll end up on the following URL (again, the actual date values may differ):

http://localhost:4000/general/2016/06/25/new-post.html

There are a few things to note here. First, the category of the blog entry is included in the URL. Personally, I don't think that's good, and you'll see how to modify this when we get to the configuration of Jekyll later. The next three items represent the date of the post. This is *not based* on the filename of the post, but on the date in the YAML. Generally you want these to agree just to make things easier to understand, but they don't need to. The final part of the URL, *new-post*, comes from the filename. Generally, this value is based on the title of the post. For example, if my post was titled "My new cat is named Sinatra!", you would use a filename of *YEAR-MONTH-DAY-my-new-cat-is-named-sinatra*. Essentially, this is a file-safe version of the title by the fact that it's lowercase and missing the punctuation from the title.

Go ahead and click on the link to open the post. You'll see an example in Figure 3-9.

Hello World!

Jun 25, 2016

This is a test!

Figure 3-9. Your new post

The layout of the post was handled by Jekyll. If you modify the front matter to tweak the title and modify the HTML, you can then reload the page and see your changes. If you used Markdown for your extension, then you'll notice that Jekyll automatically converted it into HTML as well.

A Quick Introduction to Liquid

So how exactly did Jekyll create that list of blog entries on the home page? Jekyll includes a dynamic template language called Liquid. *Liquid* is a powerful templating language that includes the ability to output simple variables, loop over lists, conditionally show content, and include other templates. A full explanation of the language is beyond the scope of this book, but luckily you won't need to be an expert at it to use it with Jekyll. Liquid has its own home page for documentation on GitHub (*https://github.com/Shopify/liquid/wiki*), which you should bookmark for easy reference while you work. You can also bookmark Jekyll Cheat Sheet (*http://jekyll.tips/jekyll-cheat-sheet/*) for Liquid tags that are specifically used in Jekyll.

Let's take a look at the home page as an example of Liquid at work. You can find the home page in *_layouts/home.html*s.

```
---
layout: default
---

<div class="home">

  <h1 class="page-heading">Posts</h1>
```

```
<ul class="post-list">
  {% for post in site.posts %}
    <li>
      <span class="post-meta">
              {{ post.date | date: "%b %-d, %Y" }}</span>

      <h2>
        <a class="post-link"
              href="{{ post.url | relative_url }}">{
              { post.title | escape }}</a>
      </h2>
    </li>
  {% endfor %}
</ul>

<p class="rss-subscribe">subscribe
<a href="{{ "/feed.xml" | relative_url }}">via
RSS</a></p>

</div>
```

I want you to notice two things in particular. First, take a look at the loop block that begins with {% for ... %}. Liquid uses {% ... %} as a marker for logic (looping and conditionals).

Next, notice how the date is displayed: {{ post.date | date: "%b %-d, %Y" }}. Liquid uses {{ ... }} when doing simple variable replacements. You can see multiple examples of this in the template. Sometimes the values are just displayed as they are: {{ post.title }}, and sometimes they are modified: {{ post.date | date: "%b %-d, %Y" }}. In the previous example, the pipe character acts like a filter—in this case doing date formatting. Later examples show a relative_url filter that—as you can probably guess—modifies a value into a relative URL for the site. (You can find all the supported Liquid filters here: *http://shopify.github.io/liquid/filters/abs/*. The additional filters Jekyll supports are documented here: *http://jekyllrb.com/docs/ templates/*.)

The variables, like site.posts, aren't a Liquid feature but come from Jekyll giving your template access to your site's content. If you open up *feed.xml*, you'll see a similar loop used to generate the RSS feed for the site. There are a whole set of variables Jekyll provides to your templates and you can find the complete list at the Jekyll Variables documentation page (*https://jekyllrb.com/docs/variables/*). Let's modify the home page to include one of the values: the post excerpt.

Within *home.html*, add the following line before the closing <li> tag:

```
{{ post.excerpt }}
```

Reload the home page and you'll notice that a portion of the blog entry now shows up on the home page, shown in Figure 3-10.

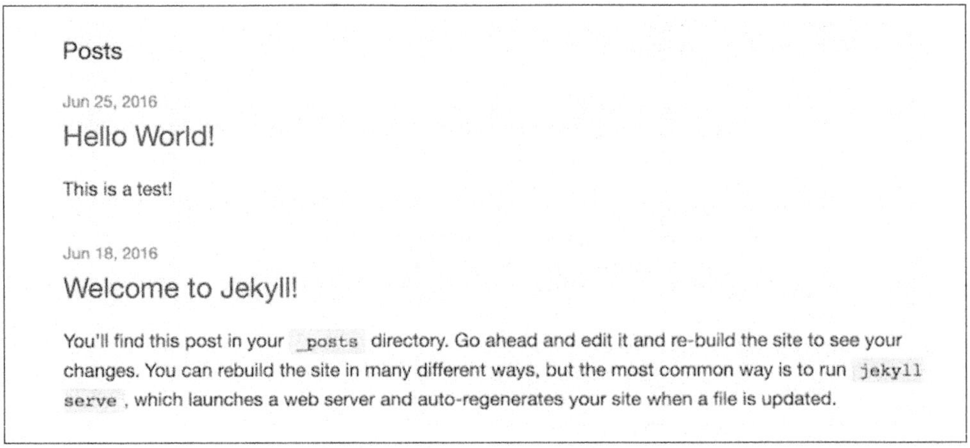

Figure 3-10. Post excerpts

So how did Jekyll create this excerpt? By default, Jekyll grabs the first paragraph of content from your post. There are multiple ways to change this, though. First, in your front matter, you can simply write your own excerpt. Or, you can define a "marker" in your post for where an excerpt should be created. For example, many blogging engines will let you write `<!--more-->` to define where the excerpt should end.

Working with Layouts and Includes

Now that you've seen how to write a post and had a quick introduction to the Liquid templating language, let's look at how Jekyll renders the content *around* your posts— the layout.

As you've already noticed, the default Jekyll site has a rather simple layout. The expectation is that you'll replace it with your own custom theme. But while the layout is simple, the actual support for working with layouts is quite involved and well-executed. Let's go over the basics.

With Jekyll, layouts are defined in the front matter of every page. If you open up any of your posts, you'll see a layout value defined in the YAML on top of the page. If you do not specify a layout value, then no layout is used.

The value specified in the front matter should *not* include an extension. So while your layout file may be called *profile.html*, you would only use the value `profile` when specifying it as your layout.

A layout file includes the contents of the file that uses it by outputting a variable called `content`. Here is an incredibly simple and short example of a layout:

```
<html>
<head></head>
```

```
<body>
{{ content }}
</body>
</html>
```

Any file using this layout would be "wrapped" with the HTML that precedes {{ con tent }} as well as the HTML that follows it.

Layout files themselves can also call other layout files. This means you can define a core, site-wide layout and then a specific layout for your blog posts. You can see an example of this in the default site produced by the Jekyll command line. Open up *post.html* in the *_layouts* folder and you'll see that it specifies `default` as the layout for itself. That means a post specifying `post` for its layout would first be wrapped by *post.html* and then *default.html*.

Finally, all of your layout files should be included in the *_layouts* folder. You get this folder by default when you create a new Jekyll site.

Of course, sometimes you may want to reuse content across a site in a "non-wrapped" format. You may simply have some text or boilerplate HTML that you need to use in multiple locations. To support this feature, Jekyll comes with an `include` command that will simply insert the contents of another file into the one currently being rendered. You can see an example of this in the default layout shown here in Example 3-2:

Example 3-2. Jekyll include default layout

```
<!DOCTYPE html>
<html>

{% include head.html %}

<body>

        {% include header.html %}

        <div class="page-content">
        <div class="wrapper">
                {{ content }}
        </div>
        </div>

        {% include footer.html %}

</body>

</html>
```

In this layout file, you can see two includes being used: one for *header.html* and one for *footer.html*. Notice that you *do* need to specify a file extension but you do *not* need to specify a folder. Jekyll will automatically look for these in the `_includes` folder. These includes can be dynamic and make use of Liquid. This comes in handy especially for things like your page title.

If you view the About page, notice that the title in your browser tab is "About". If you view source, you'll see it in the code as well: `<title>About</title>`. Where did this come from? Two places actually. First, notice the front matter for *about.md* includes a title value: `title: About`. This gets picked up by Jekyll and becomes a variable that can be used by Liquid. If you open *_includes/head.html*, you'll see this in action:

```
<title>{% if page.title %}{{ page.title | escape }}{% else
%}{{ site.title | escape }}{% endif %}</title>
```

The `site.title` variable is also something that can be tweaked. We'll discuss it later in the section "Configuring Your Jekyll Site" on page 57.

Finally, you can also call includes and pass arguments to them. Here's an example:

```
{% include youtube-video.html id="4nx7g60Ldig"}
```

In your include file, the variable `id` is referenced via the `include` scope, as demonstrated here:

```
<a href="https://www.youtube.com/watch?v={{ include.id }}">Watch video</a>
```

I hope that the benefits of layouts and includes are evident to you, but in case they aren't, it's helpful to remind ourselves of why these are such powerful features. In most sites, the layout consists of a particular set of tags that drives the look and feel for what you see. Everything from the structure (menu on the top, or menu on the right) to the design (dark green header with blue text) is consistent across the site, giving every page a uniform look and feel. Moving to static websites without an engine like Jekyll means having to repeat this code in every file, greatly increasing the amount of work required to update the design or make changes across the site. By using layouts, and includes, you're saving time (and money) implementing your site.

Adding Additional Files

While Jekyll is generally focused on creating blogs and blog posts, your site will most likely have additional pages that aren't posts. When you created your initial Jekyll site, you saw an example of this—the About page. There is nothing special about this file besides the fact that it isn't within the `_posts` folder. By simply including any HTML or Markdown file in the root of the Jekyll folder, they will automatically be parsed for their Liquid tags, wrapped in layouts, and available in the final static version of your site.

Though you have an example of this already, go ahead and create a new file in the root of the demo1 folder called *cats.html*. Example 3-3 shows the contents of this file.

Example 3-3. cats.html file contents

```
---
layout: default
title: Cats
---

<div class="home">

  <h1 class="page-heading">Cats</h1>

  <p>
  If my blog were a collection of cats instead of posts,
  I'd have {{ site.posts.size }} cats.
  </p>

</div>
```

Although this is a rather trivial example, it shows how you can create content that is totally unrelated to the blog itself (Figure 3-11). This isn't a post; it's just supporting content. And as you can see, it can contain Liquid tags. In this case, we've asked for the total number of posts. Because the file is in the root of the Jekyll folder, it will be found in the root of the domain—in this case, *http://localhost:4000/cat.html*. You're free to create any subdirectories you want of course, but obviously you want to avoid folders Jekyll uses for special purposes, like _layouts.

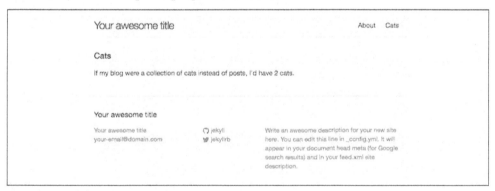

Figure 3-11. The new cat page

Did you notice how the header automatically added a link to the new page? You can actually find the code behind that logic in the include *header.html*. It is included via this logic:

```
{% for my_page in site.pages %}
    {% if my_page.title %}
    <a class="page-link"
    href="{{ my_page.url | relative_url }}">{{ my_page.title | escape }}</a>
    {% endif %}
{% endfor %}
```

This just shows again an example of the type of data Jekyll provides to your templates. In this case, you can actually ask Jekyll for a list of known pages. Since you just created a new page, Jekyll knows about it and your code can work with it.

Finally, if you don't like the URL Jekyll used for the new page and you don't want to rename the file itself, you can specify the link to use in your front matter by adding a `permalink` value. This will override the URL that's based on the filesystem.

Working with Data

Now you know the basics of creating a Jekyll site, creating content and pages, and how layouts work. It's time to kick it up a notch and work with some more powerful features. The first one we'll tackle is data files. Data files are a way to provide data to a Jekyll site in an abstract fashion. So what exactly does that mean?

Imagine for a moment that you have a simple page representing your board of directors. Now imagine that board of directors is all cats. Because—why not? Though you could build this out manually, you realize that you may want to be able to get this list of directors and use it elsewhere. Or you may want to provide multiple versions of this, such as a list of left-handed members. Jekyll provides a way for you to define a generic *data set*. This data can consist of anything you can possibly imagine. Once defined, and you'll see how that's done in a minute, you can then access this data in your blog posts, pages, layouts, and includes and use it as you see fit.

To begin, your data files should live in a folder called `_data`. This folder is *not* created by Jekyll by default, so simply create it yourself. (If you've downloaded the GitHub version of the code samples, everything in this section can be found in the `demo2` folder.)

Inside that folder, you'll then create a file that represents your data. Jekyll will use the filename as a way to reference the data, so you want to ensure that you use a sensible name. If your data is a list of cats, then your filename should be *cats.something*, where the extension defines how the data is represented. Jekyll's data feature supports YAML, JSON, and CSV files.

For this first demo, create a file called *cats.json*. This will represent a data set of cats. You can either use the code downloaded from the GitHub repo for the book or copy the content of Example 3-4. Feel free to edit the names and other properties to your liking. (In fact, we've trimmed the data set a bit in this example!)

Example 3-4. Code for cats.json file

```
[
    {
            "name":"Elvis",
            "age":4,
            "gender":"male",
            "picture":"http://placekitten.com/200/300"
    },
    {
            "name":"Sinatra",
            "age":8,
            "gender":"male",
            "picture":"http://placekitten.com/400/330"
    }
]
```

In Example 3-4, you can see two cats with four properties. Just to be clear, this is 100% arbitrary. Jekyll doesn't care what kind of data you store and how you store it. It simply makes it available to your site. The nature of the data (and what defines a cat, for example) is completely up to you.

Now that this data is defined, you can start using it in your templates. One simple example would be to list all the cats:

```
---
layout: page
title: The Board of Cats
---

<ul>
{% for cat in site.data.cats  %}
        <li>{{cat.name}}</li>
{% endfor %}
</ul>
```

At the top, you see the normal YAML front matter for a Jekyll page. Under this is an unordered list. To iterate over the cats, we "address" it using `site.data.cats`. Again, Jekyll uses the filename to create the handle you use in your code. If the filename was *furrycreaturesofevil.json*, then the reference in our pages would be `site.data.furry creaturesofevil`. For each cat, we simply output the name. Much like how Jekyll doesn't care what data you create, it doesn't care how you use it either. You're welcome to include data you may not need, or may use in the future. The result is pretty much as you expect: a list of cats (Figure 3-12).

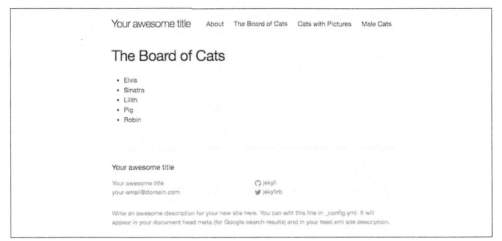

Figure 3-12. The list of cats—a cat list

Of course, you can mix it up a bit as well. Example 3-5, *male_cats.html,* shows basic filtering of the data set.

Example 3-5. Filtering the data set

```
---
layout: page
title: Male Cats
---

<ul>
{% for cat in site.data.cats  %}
        {% if cat.gender == 'male' %}
        <li>{{cat.name}}</li>
        {% endif %}
{% endfor %}
</ul>
```

And Example 3-6 shows a slightly more complex (*cats_with_pics.html*) example showing the entire data set being used:

Example 3-6. The entire data set

```
---
layout: page
title: Cats with Pictures
---

{% for cat in site.data.cats  %}
        <p>
        <img src="{{cat.picture}}"><br/>
```

```
        {{cat.name}} is a {{cat.gender}} cat and is {{cat.age}} years old.
        </p>
{% endfor %}
```

The result is absolutely lovely, as you can see in Figure 3-13. In case you're curious, those pictures come from Placekitten.com (*http://www.placekitten.com*), a placeholder image service comprised completely of cat pictures.

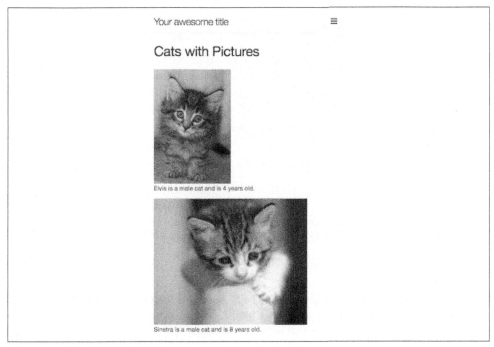

Figure 3-13. This is an even better list of cats

Configuring Your Jekyll Site

One aspect we haven't dealt with yet is configuring your Jekyll site. Jekyll can be configured at the command line via flags and by editing the *_config.yml* file. Which one you use is up to you and what your particular site needs. If you simply want to test a particular change, it makes sense to use a command line flag. If you are sure you want Jekyll to act a particular way going forward, then use the config file.

There are quite a few different options for configuration, so developers should check the documentation (*https://jekyllrb.com/docs/configuration/*), but let's consider a few simple examples of things you may want to tweak right away.

Updates to Configuration

Note that if you decide to play with a local Jekyll site while reading —and you're highly encouraged to do so—Jekyll will not notice changes to your configuration automatically. You will need to stop and restart the server to see them reflected.

`title: Your awesome title`

Used not by Jekyll but by the default layout. If you open the include *header.html,* you'll notice this: `<a class="site-title" href="{{ site.base url }}/">{{ site.title }}</a>`. The variable `site.title` comes directly from the configuration file. You can add your own variable to the configuration file and then access it via the site object. This is an example of a configuration value that doesn't necessarily drive how Jekyll operates but is used within your layouts as a sort of global variable. You can see the same thing with the `email`, `twit ter_username`, and `github_username` values. You can add or remove these as you see fit.

`port`

Used locally when testing your Jekyll server. You won't see this in your default *_config.yml.* If you don't like the default port (4000), or perhaps you want to run multiple Jekyll servers at once, you can tweak the port. You can either specify it in your config file or pass it via the command line: `jekyll server --port=4001`.

`permalink`

Used by Jekyll to determine how URLs are created for posts. While you can configure this on a per-post basis, most likely you'll want to set this up one time for the entire site. By default, Jekyll uses a permalink that includes the category of the post itself. Looking at the site used in the *demo1* folder, the URLs for a post look like this:

http://localhost:4000/general/2016/06/25/new-post.html
http://localhost:4000/jekyll/update/2016/06/18/welcome-to-jekyll.html

In the first URL, only one category was specified (general) and in the second post, two were used (jekyll and update).

While this may be fine, most sites use a URL that includes the dates only and not the categories. Jekyll lets you change this by using the `permalink` setting. Jekyll supports defining permalinks by using various tokens. The default looks like this:

`/:categories/:year/:month/:day/:title.html`

Each token is prefixed with a colon and represents data from the information about the post. Notice that the last token, `:title`, will be automatically formatted, so it is safe for a URL. To remove the category values from the links, you can simply edit your *_config.yml* file to include the new permalink value:

```
permalink: /:year/:month/:day/:title
```

You can see the complete list of tokens at Jekyll's Permalink documentation (*http://bit.ly/2ljn7r8*). While this is easy to tweak, you'll probably want to decide which style you prefer before you launch your site.

Generating a Site

You may have noticed that Jekyll constantly rebuilds your site as you work on it. It stores the static version in the subdirectory `_site`. If you want to generate a static version manually, simply run `jekyll build`. By default, it will use the current directory as the source and `_site` as the destination, but both can be changed via command-line arguments. Here's an example: `jekyll --source ../blog --destination ../output`.

Figure 3-14 shows an example of the output from the demo3 site. Note that the posts each end up in a unique folder based on the date. This is because of the changes made to the *_config.yml* file in the permalink value. If you compare this to the output from demo1, the folder structure is different.

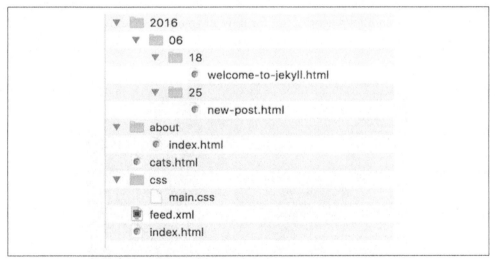

Figure 3-14. Static output from Jekyll

Building a Blog

Since Jekyll caters heavily to blogs, just creating a new Jekyll site gives you a blog out of the box. In theory, you're done and we can wrap the chapter up right here. Obviously, though, you probably won't go live with Jekyll's default look and feel for your site, so let's discuss how you can find a theme, customize it, and make it your own.

There are quite a few open source and commercial blog templates out there. It turns out that many of them come with Jekyll versions as well. One such theme, Clean Blog (*http://bit.ly/2kVRxfU*), looks great and includes both a "regular" version and a Jekyll template. Go ahead and download the Jekyll version (from the GitHub repository), unzip it, and try running it from the command line. Remember to stop any other Jekyll server you have up.

The first time you try to run the Jekyll site, you might encounter an error like the one shown in Figure 3-15:

Figure 3-15. An error from the template

What you're seeing here is the fact that the Jekyll template makes use of a *gem*, a Ruby package, as part of its plugin functionality. This is described in more detail in the docs (*https://jekyllrb.com/docs/plugins/*), but for now all you need to know is how to install the code necessary for the template. Luckily this is pretty simple: `bundle install` (Figure 3-16).

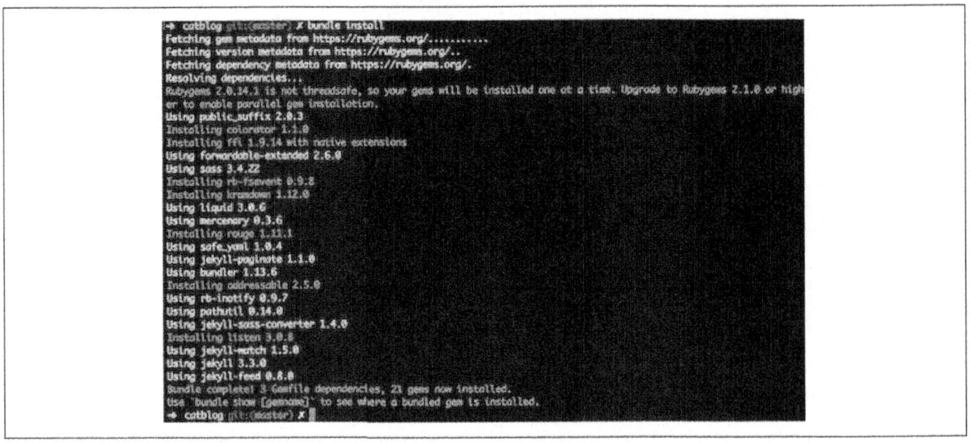

Figure 3-16. Adding the Gem required for the template

If you get an error that `bundle` isn't a valid command, then first install it using `gem install bundler`.

Once done, the blog should start up fine. But there's another hitch you may not even notice. If you try to view the blog at http://localhost:4000, where you viewed all the previous examples, you'll notice that you get an error instead. If you go back to your command-line prompt, you'll see why (Figure 3-17):

```
→  startbootstrap-clean-blog-jekyll-master jekyll s
Configuration file: /Users/raymondcamden/Downloads/startbootstrap-clean-blog-jekyll-master/_config.y
ml
             Source: /Users/raymondcamden/Downloads/startbootstrap-clean-blog-jekyll-master
        Destination: /Users/raymondcamden/Downloads/startbootstrap-clean-blog-jekyll-master/_site
  Incremental build: disabled. Enable with --incremental
         Generating...
                      done in 0.311 seconds.
  Auto-regeneration: enabled for '/Users/raymondcamden/Downloads/startbootstrap-clean-blog-jekyll-mas
ter'
 Configuration file: /Users/raymondcamden/Downloads/startbootstrap-clean-blog-jekyll-master/_config.y
ml
     Server address: http://127.0.0.1:4000/startbootstrap-clean-blog-jekyll/  ⬅
  Server running... press ctrl-c to stop.
```

Figure 3-17. See the nonstandard path?

This template uses a feature of Jekyll that lets you define a particular subdirectory for a blog. This comes in handy when a blog is a subset of your entire site. While handy, this is something we'll tweak. When you enter the correct URL, you'll see your new blog in all its glory (Figure 3-18).

Figure 3-18. The blog template in action

At this point, we have one main job: we need to modify this blog so it matches our design requirements. For example, we can replace that header image with something more appropriate. The title, too, should be changed. If you scroll to the bottom, you'll also notice various social media icons that have to change as well.

What you change, of course, depends on what you feel is necessary for your blog. You may find a template that perfect right out of the box. For now, let's focus on changing a few things to make the blog more appropriate for our subject matter, cats.

Let's begin by looking at _config.yml, shown in Example 3-7.

Example 3-7. Checking _config.yml file

```
# Site settings
title: Clean Blog
header-img: img/home-bg.jpg
email: your-email@yourdomain.com
copyright_name: Your/Project/Corporate Name
description: "Write your site description here.
It will be used as your sites meta description as well!"
baseurl: "/startbootstrap-clean-blog-jekyll"
url: "http://yourdomain.com"
twitter_username: SBootstrap
github_username:  davidtmiller
facebook_username:  IronSummitMedia
email_username:  your-email@yourdomain.com

# Google Analytics
# To enable google analytics, uncomment below line with a valid Google Tracking ID
# google_tracking_id:

# Build settings
markdown: kramdown
highlighter: rouge
permalink: pretty
paginate: 5
exclude: ["less","node_modules","Gruntfile.js","package.json","README.md"]

gems: [jekyll-paginate, jekyll-feed]
```

From top to bottom, let's make these changes:

1. Change the `title` to "*The Cat Blog*."
2. Leave `header-img` alone. We *will* be changing it, but in this case the configuration is specifying a filename. We can replace it later.
3. Change `email` to your own email.
4. Change `description` to "A blog about cats!"
5. Completely remove `baseurl`.
6. Change `url` if you want, but it need not be a real site.
7. Change `twitter_username` to your own, or keep it, but we'll keep this social link.
8. Remove `github_username` and `facebook_username`. Again, we're kind of making some arbitrary decisions here. Feel free *not* to remove them and change them to new values if you want.

9. Finally, set `email_username` to the same value you used for `email`.

You can find the final version of _config.yml_ in the code repository for the book, but go ahead and kill your Jekyll server, restart it, and see your changes (Figure 3-19).

Figure 3-19. Our cat blog is getting there!

Now let's fix that header image. While you can find any image you want, we'll make use of Placekitten.com (*https://placekitten.com/*). The config file specified the header file as *img/home-bg.jpg*. If you open that up and check the size, you'll see it is 1900 pixels wide and 872 pixels high. Using Placekitten, you can generate an image of the same size by going to this URL: *https://placekitten.com/1900/872*. On that page, simply download the graphic and save it over the existing filename. Now when you reload, you'll see your new header, shown in Figure 3-20.

Figure 3-20. That's a beautiful cat header!

Now let's change the text on the home page. You can see that the title loaded from configuration, but what about the tagline beneath it, "A Clean Blog Theme by Start Bootstrap"? If you open up *index.html*, you'll see that this is actually defined in the front matter:

```
---
layout: page
description: "A Clean Blog Theme by Start Bootstrap"
---
```

Go ahead and change that description to "A Blog about Cats", reload, and you'll see the change. Now let's do a few more tweaks. You may have noticed two links in the top of the site: About and Contact. We can't support Contact forms yet (we will learn how to do that later in the book, though), so just delete the file (*contact.html*) from the folder. Reload, and it's gone from the header. Like you saw earlier, Jekyll is actually driving this based on the files in the folder. Just removing the file is enough to remove it from the navigation.

Now open *about.html* and modify the "Lorem ipsum" text. It doesn't matter what you type, so just go ahead and change it so you can see it in action. Like the home page, this file has a description field you can change as well. Notice that this page also points to a header file (*img/about-bg.jpg*). If you want, you can change this as well. The image I used was from Placekitten (*https://placekitten.com/1200/600*) again. Figure 3-21 shows the final version of the About page from the book repository.

Figure 3-21. The cat-flavored About page

And with that, we're done with the site layout and related pages. Once again, "done" is a relative term here. You can continue to tweak the layout to your heart's content. Now let's handle the blog content. Right now there are six files in the _posts directory. Go ahead and delete all but one file. Take that last file, and rename it to match the current date and a name that's more appropriate. For example: *2016-07-23-welcome-to-my-blog.markdown*. You'll notice that the template used Markdown files for its posts. If you want to change the post to HTML, simply rename the extension as well. Open up the file, and update the front matter and text as shown in Example 3-8:

Example 3-8. Changing post to HTML from Markdown

```
---
layout:     post
title:      "Welcome to my blog!"
subtitle:   "Cats are worth blogging about!"
date:       2016-07-23 12:00:00
author:     "Raymond Camden"
header-img: "img/post-bg-06.jpg"
---
```

Everything here should be pretty standard, but note that the time isn't being used by the template, so it doesn't matter what value you set there. For the text, just type what you want. I used text from Cat Ipsum (*http://www.catipsum.com*), a "Lorem Ipsum" generator with a cat flavor. Lastly, I generated another custom cat picture, shown in Figure 3-22, from Placekitten with this URL: *https://placekitten.com/888/400.*

Figure 3-22. Our first blog post

And that's it! You could easily customize this even more, but now you're ready to launch your own cat blog. (And to be clear, this is highly recommended.)

Going Further with Jekyll

Liked what you saw in Jekyll? Here's a quick tour of some of the things we didn't cover but which may excite you even more:

- Probably one of the most powerful features is automatic pagination. Jekyll can handle correctly "sizing" the page as well as creating all of the additional files to handle showing each page of content. You also get an easy way to support adding the Previous and Next links in whatever fashion you want. You can see this in action if you add five more posts to the cat blog project created earlier. It's set to show five posts per page.
- Jekyll also has a powerful plugin system (*https://jekyllrb.com/docs/plugins/*) for adding additional functionality to your site. This can include generators (which make new files), new *tokens* you can use in your templates, and even extensions to the CLI. It's very diverse and powerful. Speaking from experience, I once had to build a plugin and even though I didn't know Ruby, it wasn't difficult to do.
- Jekyll has a concept called *collections* (*https://jekyllrb.com/docs/collections/*), which lets you define your own set of content that can act like posts and pages. This is a powerful feature that might be too much for a simple blog, but it's great that Jekyll includes this functionality.
- Finally, while we're going to talk about deploying your static sites later in the book, Jekyll is used by GitHub and their GitHub Pages feature (*https://*

pages.github.com/). GitHub Pages provides a way to publish static sites simply by committing files to your repository. If you want to host static content for your GitHub project, you can easily use Jekyll along with it. If your Jekyll site uses plugins, be sure to check GitHub's docs as they only support a subset of plugins.

For more information, see the Jekyll documentation (*https://jekyllrb.com/docs/home/*). You can also find support at the official Jekyll forums (*https://talk.jekyllrb.com/*).

## CHAPTER 4

Building a Documentation Site

Brian Rinaldi

While there are many different types of documentation sites—from hardware or software documentation to project or policy documentation—most of these sites share some common characteristics.

Characteristics of a Documentation Site

The first characteristic of a documentation site is that they tend to have multiple, and often numerous, contributors. In the case of project or policy documentation, contributors might exclusively be company employees. However, in a software world increasingly dominated by open source, many documentation sites have a large number of external contributors.

Second, a typical documentation site is fairly simple and straightforward in terms of features and design. Most of the time, the layout and design is intentionally simple and geared towards readability over style. Outside of things like comments or a runnable example, a documentation site rarely includes complex, dynamic functionality.

Third, most documentation sites change infrequently. Usually, a documentation site receives periodic significant updates with occasional minor ones in between.

While none of these characteristics is a requirement for choosing a static site, they do enable documentation sites to take advantage of the benefits of using a static site generator.

All that being said, there are some drawbacks to choosing a static site generator for building a documentation site. For one, it generally requires that a developer or development team be involved in the creation of the site and often in the regular build and deployment of updates. Also, there is no built-in authoring interface that would be comfortable for a nontechnical author/contributor. This can be a challenge if your documentation writers are used to authoring in WYSIWYG interfaces rather than markup languages like Markdown.

Overcoming the Drawbacks

It's worth noting that there are a number of ways to overcome the challenges listed here for documentation sites. For instance, the build and deployment process could be handled via services that make this a simple one-step process. Also, the editor could be improved by leveraging one of the available static-site content management systems (CMS) available. We'll discuss these options in Chapter 6.

Choosing a Generator for Your Documentation Site

Pretty much any static site generator will work for creating a documentation site. In fact, many documentation sites, including well-known projects like PhoneGap (*http://docs.phonegap.com/*) and Kendo UI (*http://bit.ly/2kVRJeN*), already use Jekyll. Many smaller software projects choose Jekyll primarily because of the built-in integration into GitHub Pages (*https://pages.github.com/*). In this chapter, however, we will use Hugo (*http://www.gohugo.io/*), a Go-based static site generator that has been rapidly growing in popularity recently.

Why choose Hugo?

The primary reason I recommend Hugo for documentation sites is that the build process is extremely fast. While this can be insignificant for smaller sites, many documentation sites can grow very large and unwieldy, making the build process a bottleneck in updating and deploying the site.

The secondary reason is that Hugo does not come preconfigured for running a blog —a format that's unsuitable for most documentation sites. This makes it easier to set up Hugo for whatever site structure you need for your documentation site without needing to restructure the default setup. In fact, Hugo even offers a number of community themes (*http://themes.gohugo.io/*) designed specifically for building a documentation site.

For the remainder of this chapter, we'll look at how to build a basic documentation site using Hugo.

Our Sample Documentation Site

We're going to build a documentation site for an esoteric programming language (*http://bit.ly/2kIrFZx*) called LOLCode (*http://lolcode.org/*). Figure 4-1 shows the home page.

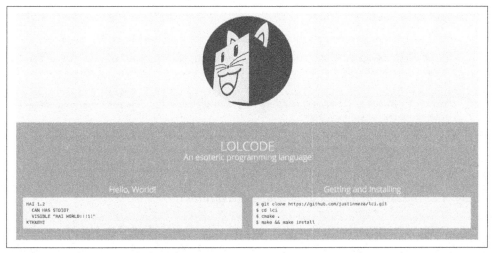

Figure 4-1. The LOLCode home page

While LOLCode is designed to be a humorous language with an intentionally difficult syntax to comprehend, it does have a full language specification (*http://bit.ly/2lIPqAt*). Right now, that language spec is a simple and boring plain-text page on GitHub, shown in Figure 4-2.

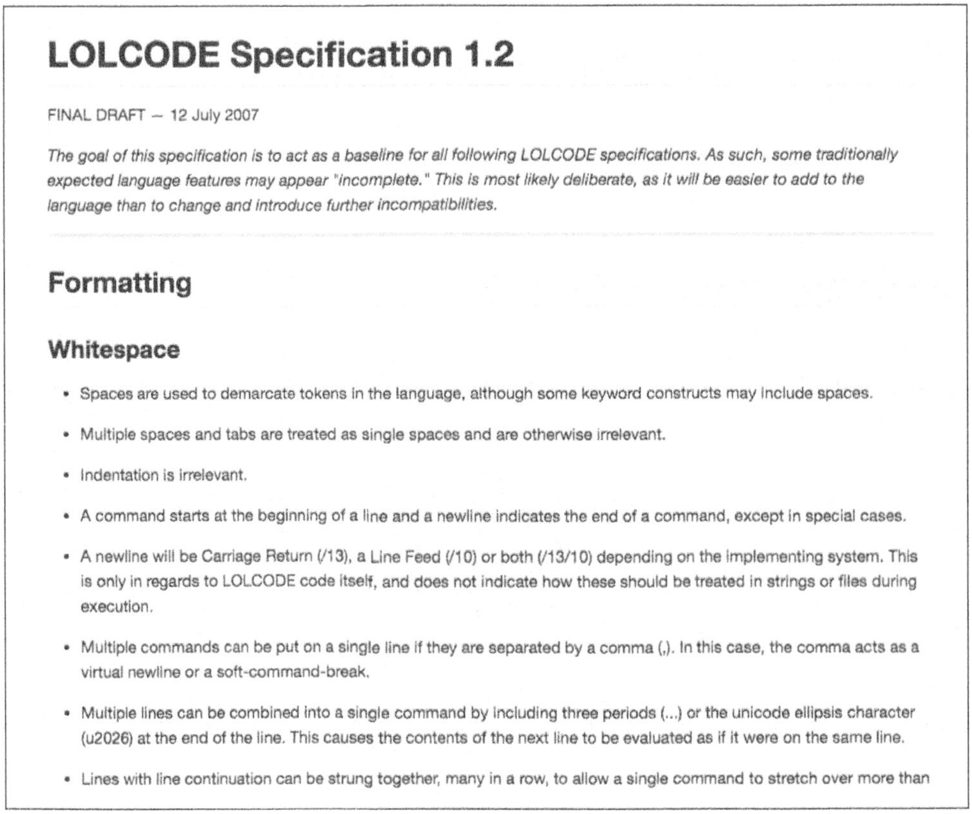

LOLCODE Specification 1.2

FINAL DRAFT — 12 July 2007

The goal of this specification is to act as a baseline for all following LOLCODE specifications. As such, some traditionally expected language features may appear "incomplete." This is most likely deliberate, as it will be easier to add to the language than to change and introduce further incompatibilities.

Formatting

Whitespace

- Spaces are used to demarcate tokens in the language, although some keyword constructs may include spaces.

- Multiple spaces and tabs are treated as single spaces and are otherwise irrelevant.

- Indentation is irrelevant.

- A command starts at the beginning of a line and a newline indicates the end of a command, except in special cases.

- A newline will be Carriage Return (/13), a Line Feed (/10) or both (/13/10) depending on the implementing system. This is only in regards to LOLCODE code itself, and does not indicate how these should be treated in strings or files during execution.

- Multiple commands can be put on a single line if they are separated by a comma (,). In this case, the comma acts as a virtual newline or a soft-command-break.

- Multiple lines can be combined into a single command by including three periods (...) or the unicode ellipsis character (u2026) at the end of the line. This causes the contents of the next line to be evaluated as if it were on the same line.

- Lines with line continuation can be strung together, many in a row, to allow a single command to stretch over more than

Figure 4-2. The existing LOLCode language specification

We're going to borrow that language spec and spice it up a little bit. Using a real spec will allow us to build an example that meets a real-world use case, even if it is still relatively simple enough to remain useful as an example.

Now, those of you who know me know that I have no design skill whatsoever (though that may still be more than Ray). To overcome this obstacle, we'll use a freely available design for a basic documentation site called DocWeb (*http://bit.ly/2kVu7Hs*). Our completed site will look like Figure 4-3.

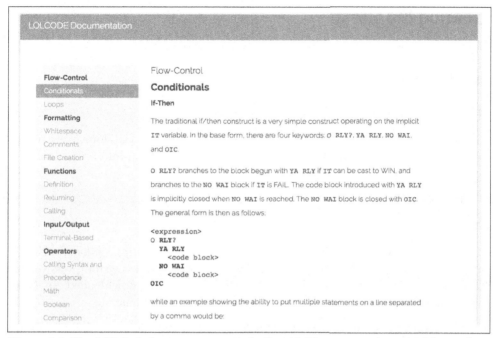

Figure 4-3. The LOLCode language spec site built with Hugo using the DocWeb template

The site itself is actually a single page with the navigation on the left being anchor links that will scroll to the appropriate section. The navigation will remain visible as the user scrolls through the long page, and the highlighted item will automatically change depending on which section the user has scrolled to.

This form of single-page documentation is common for things like language API docs or even "getting started" guides. However, even though this is a single page, it is comprised of many separate pieces of content, as we'll see shortly. In fact, if you had a larger, more complex project to document, where a single page may be unsuitable, it would be relatively easy to convert this example to use a page-per-content item rather than a single page for the entire project.

Prebuilt Hugo Themes

Although we'll be customizing our own design using the DocWeb template, Hugo has a large number of prebuilt themes that you can use, all of which can be found at *themes.gohugo.io*. There are even a few that are specifically designed for documentation sites, such as Bootie Docs (*http://themes.gohugo.io/bootie-docs/*) and Material Docs (*http://themes.gohugo.io/material-docs/*).

Creating the Site

Now that we know what we're building, let's start building it!

Installing Hugo

On Mac OS

If you are on a Mac OS, the simplest way to install Hugo is via Homebrew (*http://brew.sh/*). If you have Homebrew installed, enter the following into a terminal window.

```
brew update && brew install hugo
```

On Windows

On Windows, you'll need to download the latest release (*https://github.com/spf13/hugo/releases*) as a zip file. (Note that the latest release as of this writing was version 0.15). Hugo is simply an executable file contained within the downloaded zip. However, to use it properly, you'll need to add it to your PATH variable.

Start by creating a folder at `C:\hugo\bin`. Copy the executable into this folder (you'll want to rename it to hugo.exe.

If you are using Windows 10, follow these instructions to install Hugo:

1. Double-click the Start button and choose System.
2. Click on the "Advanced system settings" option.
3. Click the "Environment Variables…" button at the bottom of the window.
4. Choose the "Path" variable and click the Edit button.
5. Press the "New" button and type `C:\hugo\bin`.
6. Click OK, then OK again and finally OK one last time to close all the windows.

Help with Installation

If you aren't on Windows 10 or prefer not to use Homebrew, the Hugo documentation has you covered. For additional Windows options, see the "Installing on Windows (*https://gohugo.io/tutorials/installing-on-windows/*)" page. Likewise, for additional Mac options, see the "Installing on Mac (*https://gohugo.io/tutorials/installing-on-mac/*)" page.

To test that your installation is configured correctly, open the terminal or command prompt and type **hugo help**. You should receive a long list of commands and options similar to what is shown in Figure 4-4.

```
|brinaldimac:~ Rinaldi$ hugo help
hugo is the main command, used to build your Hugo site.

Hugo is a Fast and Flexible Static Site Generator
built with love by spf13 and friends in Go.

Complete documentation is available at http://gohugo.io/.

Usage:
  hugo [flags]
  hugo [command]

Available Commands:
    server      A high performance webserver
    version     Print the version number of Hugo
    config      Print the site configuration
    check       Check content in the source directory
    benchmark   Benchmark hugo by building a site a number of times.
    convert     Convert your content to different formats
    new         Create new content for your site
    list        Listing out various types of content
    undraft     Undraft changes the content's draft status from 'True' to 'False'
    import      Import your site from others.
    gen         A collection of several useful generators.
```

Figure 4-4. You can verify your install by typing the help command

Generating the Initial Site Files

Now that we've confirmed that we have Hugo installed, we can generate the initial site files using the command-line utility (CLI). Start by opening a terminal or command prompt in the folder where you would like your project to reside.

To create the folder structure and files needed to start our new Hugo site, type the following command (where *docsite* is the name of the folder that will be created):

```
hugo new site docsite
```

Hugo will generate the base files and directories necessary for a new site, as shown in Figure 4-5. Inside our *docsite* directory, we should see the following files and folders.

▶ 📁 archetypes	Today, 11:28 AM	--	Folder
📄 config.toml	Today, 11:28 AM	107 bytes	TOML file
▶ 📁 content	Today, 11:28 AM	--	Folder
▶ 📁 data	Today, 11:28 AM	--	Folder
▶ 📁 layouts	Today, 11:28 AM	--	Folder
▶ 📁 static	Today, 11:28 AM	--	Folder

Figure 4-5. The default files and directories generated by Hugo

At the moment, all of the directories are empty. Unlike many other static site generators, Hugo does not generate a default theme/layout or any dummy content. Let's start with configuring the site.

Configuring the Hugo Site

By default, Hugo uses TOML (*https://github.com/toml-lang/toml*) for configuration, but you can choose to use YAML (*http://yaml.org/*) if you prefer. The site configuration is located in the *config.toml* file within the root directory of the site. It contains only a few default values:

```
baseurl = "http://replace-this-with-your-hugo-site.com/"
languageCode = "en-us"
title = "My New Hugo Site"
```

These values should be fairly self-explanatory. Because we don't have a real URL, we'll just set the `baseurl` value to an empty string for local testing.

```
baseurl = ""
languageCode = "en-us"
title = "LOLCODE Documentation"
```

One important aspect of a documentation site for a language like LOLCode is code highlighting. There are multiple options for code highlighting in a Hugo site, but the standard solution is to do server-side code highlighting (i.e., the highlighting is added during the build phase) with Pygments (*http://pygments.org/*).

To get Pygments working, we need to have Python installed. If you don't already have it, you can download the proper version here (*https://www.python.org/downloads/*) (if you are on Windows, I suggest that you choose the option to add Python to your PATH during installation).

Once Python is installed, open a new terminal or command prompt window and install Pygments.

```
pip install Pygments
```

If you want to test that Pygments installed correctly, enter `pygmentize -h` via the command line. This should print out the Pygments command-line help documentation.

Now that Pygments is installed, let's configure Hugo to use it. We'll add the following to our *config.toml* file.

```
pygmentsStyle = "colorful"
pygmentsUseClasses = false
pygmentsCodeFences = true
```

The first option chooses one of Pygments' default styles for the code coloring. The second tells Pygments to add the code colors directly rather than depend on the *pygments.css* file. The third will allow us to use GitHub style code fences (*http://bit.ly/2miw1Tm*) in our Markdown to set code blocks and the language to use for highlighting. A GitHub style code block looks like this:

```
```javascript
// my JavaScript code here
```
```

Hugo offers more options for code syntax highlighting than we're discussing here. For details on those, visit the Hugo syntax highlighting documentation (*https://gohugo.io/ extras/highlighting/*).

Client-Side Code Coloring

One thing to consider, depending on the size of your site, is that the server-side code coloring shown here via Pygments can significantly impact build times. If this could be an issue for your site, you might consider using one of the client-side code coloring options (*http://bit.ly/2lCWxK4*) like Highlight.js or Prism.

We're done with what we need in the configuration file. Of course, there are a ton of other options available when building a site with Hugo. You can view the full list of configuration options in the Hugo configuration documentation (*https://gohugo.io/ overview/configuration/*). For now, however, let's move on to adding content and creating a layout.

Adding Content

In my opinion, one of the benefits of Hugo is that it is not very prescriptive about how you organize or name your content. Content is typically in the */content* folder, but beyond that, it's up to you how you handle things from there. In our case, our final content will actually all be rendered in a single page, so the organization isn't terribly important.

As with most static site generators, Hugo natively supports content written in Markdown. However, it also supports two other markup languages: AsciiDoc (*http://ascii doc.org/*) (via AsciiDoctor) and reStructuredText (*http://bit.ly/2kIxJRJ*). For our documentation site, we'll use Markdown.

Rather than have us write or convert all the LOLCode documentation here, I've provided a zip file containing all of the Markdown files. Simply download (*http://bit.ly/ 2kVNSyA*) and unzip it within the */content* folder of your Hugo site. All of the Markdown files should end up within a directory of */content/lolcode*.

Converting to Markdown

Rather than rewrite all of the LOLCode documentation to the Markdown format, I chose to use a converter. Thankfully, there are a number of converters available. To convert HTML to Markdown, I often use to-markdown (*https://domchristie.github.io/*

---

to-markdown/). To convert rich text to Markdown, I'll use Mark It Down (*http://markitdown.medusis.com/*). Finally, to convert Word documents to Markdown, I'll use Word to Markdown Converter (*http://word-to-markdown.herokuapp.com/*).

It's important to note, however, that in the case of this last converter, you'll need to do some manual cleanup both before (I usually remove images as they get Base64 encoded) and after (some headers and other formatting don't translate perfectly). Nonetheless, if you need to convert any document to Markdown, these tools can save you a significant amount of time.

As is typical for static site generators, Hugo uses front matter at the beginning of each content document. Essentially, *front matter* is metadata about that particular piece of content, including everything from the title and publish date to the URL and categories. By default, front matter is written in TOML, but YAML and JSON are also allowed if you prefer.

The easiest way to create a new post and ensure that it has the necessary front matter is to use the command line. Assuming that you are in the root of your site, you can simply enter the following command to create a new post named "welcome to my blog."

```
hugo new welcome-to-my-blog.md
```

The generated post will have front matter that looks like the following:

```
+++
date = "2016-06-07T19:30:29-04:00"
draft = true
title = "welcome to my blog"

+++
```

The `date` is a timestamp that will be used to determine the publish date of the post. The `draft` key indicates that this post is not yet published; you can set this to false or remove it to take the post out of draft status. Finally, the `title` is, obviously, the title of the blog post or content.

Since we've already added our content, we don't need to create a new content item (so delete the post if you created it). But let's take a look at the metadata in our documentation content, as it includes some items not in the default front matter.

```
+++
date = "2016-05-05T08:41:21-04:00"
draft = true
title = "Arrays"
categories = ["Types"]
categories_weight = 6
+++
```

We've already discussed the `date`, `draft`, and `title` values (as you can see, this is the documentation covering arrays in LOLCode). However, we've added some taxonomy via the `categories` value. This value can contain an array of categories, but in this case, we've only added one for Types. As you'll see when we create the layout, we're going to use this categories value to group our documentation (in this case, an Array is a data type, thus the category Types).

The `categories_weight` value also helps us to organize the way we will display the content on the page. In this case, we want certain content to come before other content within the Types category. The value here indicates that we want Arrays to be the sixth item in the order of the content within the Types category.

There are a lot of additional front matter metadata values that you can add to your Hugo content. Refer to the documentation (*https://gohugo.io/content/front-matter/*) for full details.

Required Front Matter in Hugo

There's some discrepancy between the Hugo documentation on front matter (*https://gohugo.io/content/front-matter/*) and the reality of front matter. The documentation indicates that title, date, description, and taxonomies are all required. However, as we discussed, Hugo doesn't include either description or taxonomies when it generates content for you, and I've never found Hugo to error when either of these keys is missing.

Creating the Layout

So, our site is configured and has content, but if we were to ask Hugo to serve it and open it in a browser, we'd get nothing. Why? Well, there is no layout to tell Hugo how to display the content.

As we discussed earlier, we aren't going to use a prebuilt theme in this case but rather will create our own layout using DocWeb (*http://bit.ly/2kVu7Hs*) as a template. To start, we need to download that template and place the zip in a temporary location. So go ahead and do that.

Now that we've unzipped the DocWeb layout, let's start moving some of the assets over to our LOLCode documentation site. First, let's copy the css, img, and js folders into */static/assets* within our Hugo site. Placing files in the static directory will copy them over to the generated site without processing them—essentially leaving them as is.

Next, copy *index.html* from the DocWeb files and place it under the */layouts* directory within our Hugo site. At this point, we technically have a home page layout (and that will be the only page for this site), but it's all in a single HTML file and the content in Hugo isn't populating. Let's fix that.

Go Templates

By default, Hugo uses the Go Template language for templates, but it also natively supports Amber (*https://github.com/eknkc/amber*) and Ace (*https://github.com/yosssi/ace*) templates. We'll cover some of the basics of creating Go Templates here but if you want a full overview, the Hugo documentation provides a great introduction (*https://gohugo.io/templates/go-templates/*), or you can review the official Go Template documentation (*https://golang.org/pkg/html/template/*).

We'll start by creating some *partials*, which are essentially includes. These allow us to break the template into reusable parts, making them easier to maintain.

Let's create a new folder under */layouts* called *partials* and create a file named *head.html*. Then take the <head> portion of *index.html* and copy it into the new *head.html* document. Back in *index.html*, place the following code where the <head> used to be.

```
{{ partial "head.html" . }}
```

Within *layouts/partials/head.html*, let's add some dynamic site data. First, let's clean the head up a bit by removing the <link> for RSS (of course, you can make an RSS file for your site using Hugo; we won't do that here because our demo is a fixed set of documentation rather than a site with regular updates) and the stylesheet for *prettify.css* (Prettify is a code highlighting tool and we've already configured Hugo to handle our code highlighting).

Next, let's replace the existing hardcoded site title with the site title we defined earlier in the site configuration file.

```
<title>{{ .Site.Title }}</title>
```

Finally, let's modify the link to the stylesheet to reference the base URL of the site to ensure that the reference URL is always correct.

```
<link rel="stylesheet" href="{{ .Site.BaseURL }}assets/css/style.css">
```

Both `Title` and `BaseURL` are site variables that Hugo makes available to use within our templates. You can find a full list of them in the Hugo documentation (*http://bit.ly/2miDYIx*).

Your completed *head.html* partial should look something like this:

```
<head>
    <title>{{ .Site.Title }}</title>
    <meta charset="utf-8">
    <meta name="description" content="">
    <meta name="HandheldFriendly" content="True">
    <meta name="MobileOptimized" content="320">
    <meta name="viewport" content=
      "initial-scale=1.0, minimum-scale=1.0, maximum-scale=1.0,
        user-scalable=no">
    <link href="http://fonts.googleapis.com/css?family=Raleway:700,300" rel=
      "stylesheet" type="text/css">
    <link rel="stylesheet" href="{{ .Site.BaseURL }}assets/css/style.css">
</head>
```

It's a good idea to split out portions of your site into partials such as this one, which can be easily reused within additional templates across your site. For example, we could also cut the footer portion of the template and place it into a *layout/partials/footer.html* file.

```
<section class="vibrant centered">
  <div class="">
    <h4> This documentation template is provided by <
    a href="http://www.frittt.com" target="_blank">Frittt Templates</a>.
    You can download and use this template for free. If you have
    used this template, please pay the developer's effort by
    Tweeting, sharing on Facebook, social mention or with a
    linkback. Enjoy! :)</h4>
  </div>
</section>
<footer>
  <div class="">
    <p> &copy; Copyright LOLCODE. All Rights Reserved.</p>
  </div>
</footer>
```

In place of the footer above, we'll add {{ partial "footer.html" }} within *layouts/index.html*.

Before we move on, let's fix one last thing in our *layouts/index.html* file. At the very bottom of the page are some script tags. Let's add the .Site.BaseURL to the ones we need (i.e., *jquery.min.js* and *layout.js*) and remove the two tags for *prettify.js* (again, we're not utilizing this for code coloring). Our scripts should look like this now.

```
<script src="{{ .Site.BaseURL }}assets/js/jquery.min.js"></script>
<script src="{{ .Site.BaseURL }}assets/js/layout.js"></script>
```

Once you've done this, you'll also want to open *static/js/layout.js* and remove the call to prettyPrint(); at the bottom of the file to avoid generating JavaScript errors.

Let's create one last partial for our template to encompass the site navigation. This one will be a little more complex as we'll want Hugo to dynamically populate the navigation based upon our content.

First, copy out the portion of HTML code in *layouts/index.html,* starting with the opening `<ul class="docs-nav">` and ending with the closing `</ul>` tag, and place it into a new file named *layouts/partials/nav.html.* Make sure to add a `{{ partial "nav.html" . }}` where the `<ul>` block used to be in *layouts/index.html.*

As you can see by examining the code for the existing, hard-coded navigation items, there are two levels of navigation elements. There are section headers that are bolded, but not clickable. For example:

```
<li>Getting Started</li>
```

And navigation elements which are clickable. For example:

```
<li><a href="#welcome" class="cc-active">Welcome</a></li>
```

If you recall, each of the content items we added had a category defined under `cate gories` in the front matter, as well as a `categories_weight`. We'll use the categories as the section headers. Then we'll place each content item within that category as a clickable navigation item, the order being determined by the `categories_weight`.

Start by deleting all but the first section header (i.e., Getting Started) and first navigation item (i.e., Welcome). Now, let's loop through all of the available categories defined by our site content. Hugo has a site variable called `.Site.Taxonomies.cate gories` that contains a structure (technically called a map in the Go language) of all of the site's categories. To loop through this structure, we're going to use the `range` keyword. Here's what the loop looks like.

```
<ul class="docs-nav">
    {{ range $name, $taxonomy := .Site.Taxonomies.categories }}
    <li><strong>{{ $name | title }}</strong></li>
        <li><a href="#welcome" class="cc-active">Welcome</a></li>
    {{ end }}
</ul>
```

In this code, `$name` is the key value from the map (`.Site.Taxonomies.categories`) and `$taxonomy` is the value, which, in this case, will be another map containing all the content within that category. Within the section header list element, we are outputting the value of the key.

The use of the pipe is something special in Go templates. In this case, we are saying to use a Hugo template function (*https://gohugo.io/templates/functions/*) to title-case the value of the `$name` variable.

Pipes in Hugo

Pipes can be utilized in more complex fashions, which you can learn about in the Hugo documentation (*https://gohugo.io/ templates/go-templates/#pipes*).

Now let's loop through and create the links to the pages within each category.

```
<ul class="docs-nav">
    {{ range $name, $taxonomy := .Site.Taxonomies.categories }}
    <li><strong>{{ $name | title }}</strong></li>
    {{ range $taxonomy.Pages }}
        {{ if ne .Title "" }}
        <li><a href="#{{ .LinkTitle | urlize }}" class="cc-active">
          {{ .Title }}</a></li>
        {{ end }}
    {{ end }}
    {{ end }}
</ul>
```

The $taxonomy variable makes a number of useful information available to output on our page. In this case, we are interested in iterating over .Pages, which has all of the pages in each given category. Within that loop, we are making sure the value of any given page's title is not empty (i.e., if ne .Title "" where ne indicates "not equal"). This is because there is one piece of content that we want to output on the page (*about_types.md*) that we do not want included in the navigation, so we've left the title off.

Since our final template will be a single page, each navigation item links to an anchor rather than a separate page. Thus, we've used another Hugo template function, urlize (*http://bit.ly/2ljpQ3X*), to convert any spaces in the page   variable .LinkTitle to dashes. Finally, within the link, we output the title of the content via .Title.

Now, let's try to run our site to see what we've done so far. Make sure that you've saved all the files, including *nav.html*. Open a terminal or command prompt window within the folder of the documentation site and enter:

```
hugo server --buildDrafts
```

The --buildDrafts flag is necessary because all of our posts are still in draft mode (i.e., draft = true in the front matter). It tells Hugo to build all our posts, including those in draft mode.

Changing the Draft Status

You can manually take a post out of draft simply by changing the draft flag in the front matter. However, you can also do so via the command line. For example, the following command will take the arrays post out of draft status:

```
hugo undraft content/lolcode/arrays.md
```

Opening *http://localhost:1313* (the default server URL for Hugo) in a browser, we should now see a site that looks like Figure 4-6:

Figure 4-6. Our documentation site with dynamic navigation added

Our navigation is now outputting correctly, but the links don't lead anywhere because we still only have hardcoded content. Let's fix that (but, go ahead and leave the site open in your browser; Hugo will automatically refresh it as you save changes).

Open *layouts/index.html*. Within the `<div class="docs-content">` block, erase all but the first few lines. You should be left with the following:

```
<div class="docs-content">
    <h2> Getting Started</h2>
    <h3 if="welcome"> Welcome</h3>
    <p> Are you listening to your customers?</p>
</div>
```

We'll do the same loop here as we did for the navigation, but, in this case, we'll actually output the full content (i.e., `.Content`) of each post. The only other difference here is that we did not include the if statement that skipped content without a title, as we now want that content outputted.

```
<div class="docs-content">
  {{ range $name, $taxonomy := .Site.Taxonomies.categories }}
      <h2>{{ $name | title }}</h2>
    {{ range $taxonomy.Pages }}
        <h3 id="{{ .LinkTitle | urlize }}">{{ .Title }}</h3>
        {{ .Content }}
        <hr>
    {{ end }}
  {{ end }}
</div>
```

Once you save this page, Hugo will automatically regenerate the site files and refresh the open browser window with your finished site (Figure 4-7).

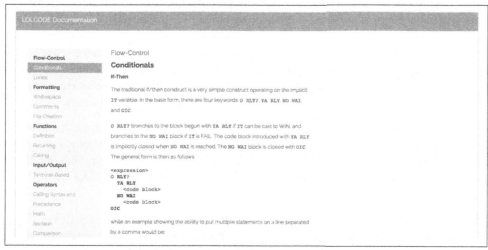

Figure 4-7. The completed LOLCode documentation site

Clicking on any of the links in the navigation should now correctly scroll to the appropriate section of the page. You should also notice that code blocks are appropriately colored.

Congrats! You're done with your first documentation site built with Hugo. The completed code for this sample can be found on the GitHub repository for this book (*http://bit.ly/2kVUGfH*).

The Scrolling Navigation

If you've tested the page we built, you may notice that some of the navigation items fall off the page and aren't visible until the entire page is scrolled to the bottom. This has to do with some JavaScript code in *static/js/layout.js* that is designed to have the navigation remain statically positioned as the user scrolls the page. Obviously, this is a bit of a flaw in the design of the DocWeb template when utilized for longer single-page documentation sites. The completed demo of this mitigates this issue through some tweaks to the Java-Script (*http://bit.ly/2lD9Rym*), though it can still be improved, in particular to account for the speed of the user's scroll.

To generate the completed site files, use the command line (note that we're still using the `buildDrafts` flag since our content is still in draft mode):

```
hugo --buildDrafts
```

Going Further

Obviously, there are many different formats you can use for a documentation site. In this particular sample project, the documentation was made up of primarily short content, which made it a very good candidate for a single page with anchors. However, if your project has long-form documentation, it would make more sense to use individual content pages. To do this, you need to add a template for the individual posts as *layouts/_default/single.html*. Of course, you could reuse the partials for the head, navigation, and footer, making it easier to build this template quickly.

One thing worth noting here for anyone looking to convert an existing documentation project to Hugo is that there are a number of converters (*https://gohugo.io/tools/*) available. These include converters from popular static site generators like Jekyll but also from dynamic site engines and content management systems like WordPress, Ghost, and Drupal.

Honestly, the toughest challenge you're likely to run into when choosing to use Hugo, or any static site generator for your documentation site, is writing content in Markdown. While developers may be comfortable writing in Markdown, many documentation writers are unfamiliar with it. Fortunately, the support for Markdown in existing or standalone tools keeps getting more robust, even if it is typically not the WYSIWYG experience many writers will be most comfortable in. Also, it's worth noting that there are a number of third-party frontends (*https://gohugo.io/tools/#fron tends*) for Hugo that aim to create an experience more similar to writing in WordPress or other content management systems.

Finally, there's a lot more that you can do with Hugo than was covered in this chapter. Thankfully, Hugo has extensive and detailed documentation (*https://gohugo.io/over view/introduction/*) (among the best of any static site generator, in my opinion).

CHAPTER 5

Adding Dynamic Elements

Raymond Camden

Now that you've made the decision to use a static site generator (woo!), you may discover that you've forgotten one little detail that seems to require a dynamic application server of some sort. Perhaps you have a contact form. Maybe you want to add discussions to your blog. Does this mean you've made a horrible mistake and have to revert everything you worked on? Of course not!

Multiple different services exist that enable you to add dynamic features back to your site. In some cases, it is nearly impossible for the end user to tell that anything "special" is being done at all. To them, it simply appears as if your site is doing whatever it needs to on the backend, when in reality you're still using simple static files.

In this chapter, we'll discuss how to add dynamic elements back in to your static site. We'll focus on:

- Forms
- Comments
- Search

We'll also discuss some other options for data types, like events and generic sets of data.

Handling Forms

Since the dawn of the web itself, forms have been an integral part of how users interact with your site. Moving to a static site doesn't make forms themselves magically stop working. They still render. You can still interact with them using JavaScript. But if you want the form to do something on a server or to communicate with someone else, then you'll be out of a luck when using a static site. Luckily, a number of options exist for adding basic form processing to your site. Let's look at a few of them.

Wufoo Forms

Let's get one thing out of the way first. Wufoo (*http://www.wufoo.com*) is the most expensive of all the options we'll cover in this chapter (Figure 5-1). However, it has an *incredibly* powerful form builder that can be very easy for nonprogrammers to use. This allows your clients to edit forms without having to go through you or deploy a new version of the static site.

Figure 5-1. Wufoo's website

At the time of writing, Wufoo offers a free tier that includes three forms and 100 responses. That's probably enough for a small site, but most will probably want to use the lowest paid option, Ad Hoc, which includes 10 forms and 500 entries. You can find higher tiers and current pricing on their site (*http://www.wufoo.com/pricing/1/*).

Go ahead and sign up for a free account, and in the form manager, click the New Form button to create a new form (Figure 5-2).

Untitled Form
No Fields! You should add a field.
Add Field

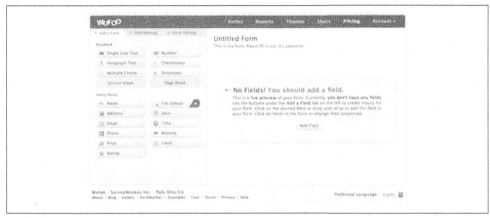

Figure 5-2. Beginning to create a new form

Next, simply drag and drop fields to create your form. Along with basic fields (text, multiple choice, etc.), Wufoo has shortcuts for common things like names (including first and last name fields) and email addresses. Figure 5-3 shows a simple contact form created by dragging and dropping the Name, Email, and Paragraph Text fields.

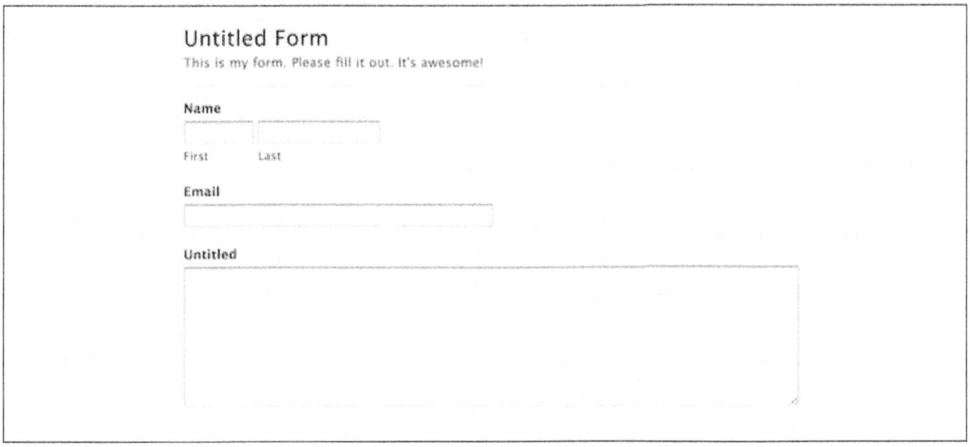
Untitled Form
This is my form. Please fill it out. It's awesome!
Name
First
Last
Email
Untitled

Figure 5-3. The first version of the contact form

Notice that the form is kind of generic. Each part of the form can be edited to provide customized text. Simply click a field or block of text, and a new editor will appear, as shown in Figure 5-4:

Figure 5-4. Editing the top portion of the form

Figure 5-5 shows the form after customizing the top portion and the paragraph text field:

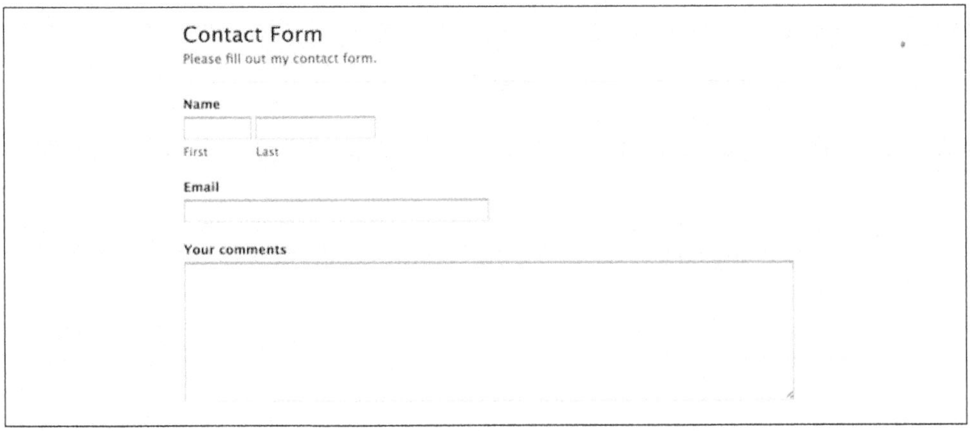

Contact Form
Please fill out my contact form.

Name

First   Last

Email

Your comments

Figure 5-5. The customized form

When you're done, save the form, and Wufoo will offer a method to share it. You can test the form via a custom URL or embed it (via JavaScript, iframe, or even Word-Press). For now, choose the JavaScript embed and click the Copy Code option. See Figure 5-6.

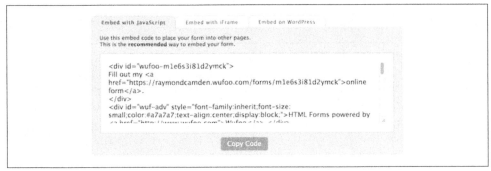

Figure 5-6. The embed code for your new form

Now that you've got the embed code, you can simply copy and paste it into any simple web page. In the source code for this book, you can find an example of the form just created in the ch5/forms folder, named *wufoo1.html*. You are welcome to try running the file as is, but since this particular example uses the free tier, you won't be able to see any of the responses. We encourage you to replace the embed with your own code from the Wufoo form editor (Figure 5-7 shows the final form). In order to make it easier, the file uses a comment:

```
<!-- Wufoo embed here -->
...
<!--- End Wufoo embed -->
```

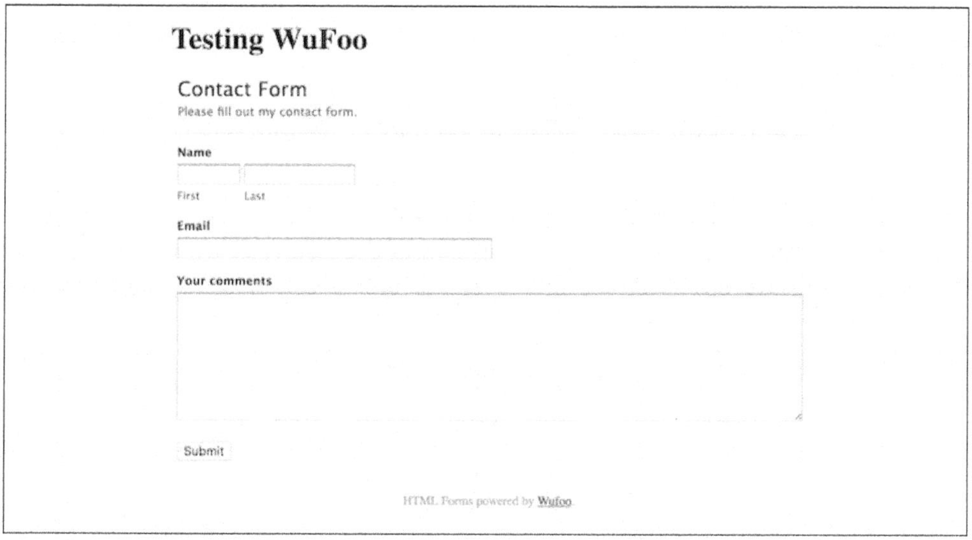

Figure 5-7. The live form

Unless you specifically said so while editing the form, nothing will be required. Also, when you submit the form, you'll end up on the Wufoo website. You can change this back in your form submission settings, shown in Figure 5-8.

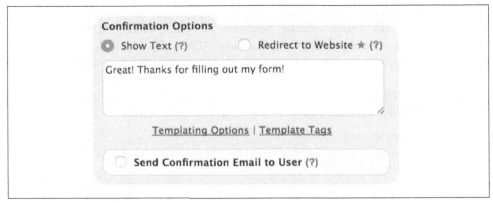

Figure 5-8. Form submission settings

The most likely option you will use here is "Redirect to Website" to send users back to your site.

When submitted, results will be available in the form manager. You can select your form, click on the entries, and get a tabular view of the results. Selecting an entry will give you the values from the submission as well as some other metadata about the form (Figure 5-9).

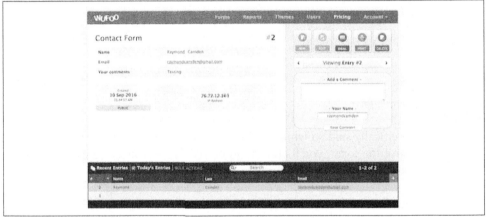

Figure 5-9. Details of the form submission

You probably also want to get the form submission emailed to you. Back in the form manager, click the Edit link to add notifications. On this page, shown in Figure 5-10, you can set up both email notifications and even an SMS message!

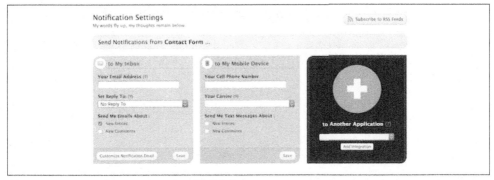

Figure 5-10. Notification settings for Wufoo

There's a lot more to Wufoo than we'll cover here. As we said in the beginning of the chapter, this is not the cheapest option but its power and ease of use are easily worth the price in most cases.

Google Docs Forms

Google Docs has become a ubiquitous method to work on documents, spreadsheets, and slide decks online and in a multiuser environment. Over the past few years, it has become a serious competitor to office suites like Microsoft Office and Apple's iWork. One feature many people don't know about is the ability to design a form. Even better —it's a free service you can use for your static site. Assuming you've got a Google account (and don't we all), simply open your browser to *https://docs.google.com/ forms/* (Figure 5-11).

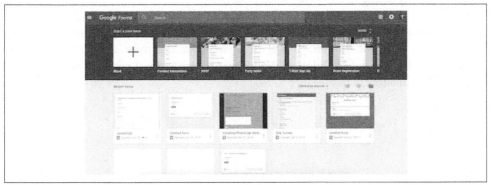

Figure 5-11. The Google Forms website

You'll see a number of templates, including one for a contact form, but go ahead and create a blank one so you can see the process of creating your own form (Figure 5-12).

Figure 5-12. A blank Google Form

By default, you are automatically editing the first question. You can change the text, question type, and other properties by using the various options on the page itself. Figure 5-13 shows the form after the first field has been changed to a short-answer, required field with a new label.

Figure 5-13. Beginning to create the contact form

You can add more fields by using the menu to the right of the form. Note that validation options are a bit hidden. To get to them, click the three dots to the right of Required and select data validation. Validating an email field requires selecting Text and then Email address (see Figure 5-14).

Figure 5-14. Adding a specific validation rule to a field

When you've gotten the form to your liking, you can preview it in your browser. Note that you don't have to add a submit button. Google does that for you (see Figure 5-15).

Figure 5-15. The contact form in action

Once you've gotten your form to your liking, actually using it is a bit weird. You need to click the SEND button on top. This is also where you'll find the embed options for the form, shown in Figure 5-16.

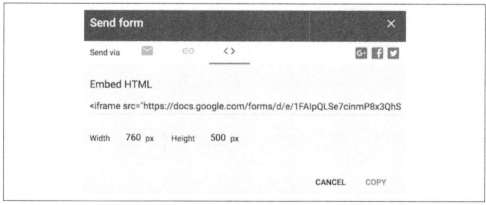

Figure 5-16. Reaching the embed options for Google Forms

As before, copy the code into your HTML file in your static site, and you're good to go. You can find an example of this in the source code for the book: *ch5/forms/ google1.html*. Figure 5-17 shows the form in a simple HTML page.

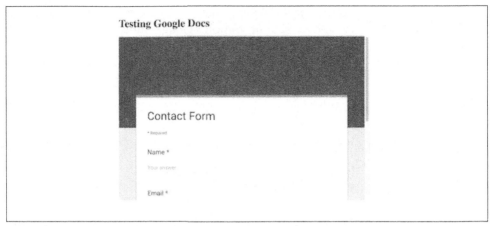

Figure 5-17. The embedded form

Notice how the iframe isn't necessarily sized correctly by default. You can customize this in the embed options and, unfortunately, you'll need to guess a few times to get it just right.

Once submitted, the user is presented with a simple message (that can be customized) and results will be made available back in the Google Form editor, shown in Figure 5-18.

Figure 5-18. Google Form responses

Email notifications are possible, but a bit weird. You'll use the "Add Ons" link on top to add notifications. It isn't just an option, but an optional extra. Once you've done that, you can tell Google to notify you. Once cool thing is that it can batch responses. This could be useful for a busy form. Figure 5-19 shows the completed form.

Figure 5-19. Setting up notifications

Formspree

Our next option is a service that's actually specifically built for static sites, Formspree (*https://formspree.io/*). How easy is Formspree? Let's look at an example. Begin with a form:

```
<form method="post">

    <p>
    <label for="name">Name: </label>
    <input type="text" name="name" id="name">
    </p>

    <p>
    <label for="email">Email: </label>
    <input type="email" name="email" id="email">
    </p>

    <p>
    <label for="comments">Comments: </label>
    <textarea name="comments" id="comments"></textarea>
    </p>
```

```
<input type="submit" value="Send Comments">

</form>
```

This is a simple form with three fields. There is no action attribute specified. To enable Formspree support, simply change the action to `https://formspree.io/someemail@some.domain`, where `someemail@some.domain` is your email address. Here is a real example (this can be found in *ch5/forms/formspree1.html*):

```
<form action="https://formspree.io/raymondcamden@gmail.com" method="post">
```

And literally—that's it. Open the form (after editing the action value to use your own email address), fill it out, and hit Submit. See Figure 5-20.

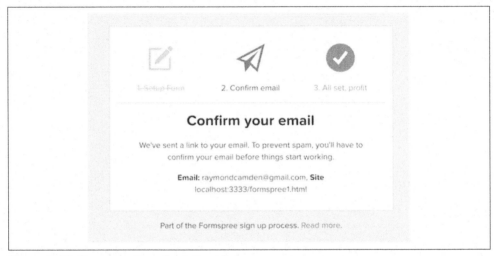

Figure 5-20. Formspree's confirmation dialog

Figure 5-20 shows a one-time security feature in which Formspree requests that you confirm that you want to get email from the service. They do this for every unique referrer URL and email address but only once. Click the confirmation link in your email and submit the form again. Now you'll see the success message shown in Figure 5-21:

Figure 5-21. Formspree's success message

There's no signup. No cost (for the first 1,000 submissions per month). It's as simple as that. Of course, you'll probably want to use a custom response. You can do that by simply adding a hidden form field (*ch5/forms/formspree2.html*):

```
<input type="hidden" name="_next" value="http://localhost:3333/thanks.html" />
```

Now when you submit the form, Formspree will send the user back to the URL provided in the value. (Note that Formspree will require you to validate the email again because this is a new file and URL that's sending the form.)

You can even customize the subject by modifying—yes—another hidden form field:

```
<input type="hidden" name="_subject" value="My Site's Comment Form" />
```

Formspree is truly an incredibly simple and powerful form service for static sites. As stated, the free tier includes 1,000 emails a month, which is incredibly generous. You can read about additional features on Formspree's website (*https://formspree.io/*).

Adding a Comment Form to Camden Grounds

Now that we've seen a few examples of how to add forms to a static site, let's update the earlier HarpJS-based demo site Camden Grounds to support a contact form. If you've downloaded the code for this book from the GitHub repository, you can find an updated version of the demo site in *ch5/forms/camdengrounds* (*http://bit.ly/2ljtYAR*). The modifications to support a form are as follows:

1. The top and bottom menus were modified to add a link to *contact.html*. This is done in the *_layout.ejs* file. If you skipped over Chapter 2, you should quickly give it a read to become familiar with the basics of Harp.
2. Then a contact form was added, named *contact.ejs*.
3. When Formspree is done processing the form, we want it to return to another new file, *thanks.ejs*.

4. Finally, some minor CSS tweaks were made to the site. Note that the styling in the demo is not spectacular. Blame the developer (me!), not Harp or Formspree.

Let's begin by looking at the contact form.

```
<div id="figure">
        <img src="images/headline-about.jpg" alt="Image">
        <span>Tell us your thoughts!</span>
</div>
<div>

        <div class="contactForm">

        <form action="https://formspree.io/raymondcamden@gmail.com"
          method="post">

                <% if(environment == "production") { %>
                <!--
                        NOTE THIS IS NOT A REAL URL!
                        Obviously someone may buy the domain
                          and put something naughty.
                -->
                <input type="hidden" name="_next"
                value="http://www.camdengrounds.com/thanks.html" />
                <% } else { %>
                <input type="hidden" name="_next"
                value="http://localhost:9000/thanks.html" />
                <% } %>

                <p>
                <label for="name">Name: </label>
                <input type="text" name="name" id="name">
                </p>

                <p>
                <label for="email">Email: </label>
                <input type="email" name="email" id="email">
                </p>

                <p>
                <label for="comments">Comments: </label><br/>
                <textarea name="comments" id="comments"></textarea>
                </p>

                <input type="submit" value="Send Comments">

        </form>

        </div>
</div>
```

For the most part, this is just a vanilla form. We made things a bit fancy by making using an advanced Harp feature, the `environment` variable. This lets us detect if we're running locally via the Harp server or using the compiled, static version. This way, we can submit the form both on our development machine as well as on the live site. (And as the source code says, we're using a fake domain that's fake as of this moment but may not be fake at the time of publication. Be careful!)

Figure 5-22 shows the new contact form in the site. (And again, the CSS could be a bit nicer!)

Figure 5-22. The new Camden Grounds contact form

And that's it! The nice thing about Formspree is how simple it is to integrate it into your static site. Don't forget that when you publish your site, you want to immediately fill out the form so Formspree can confirm your address the first time.

Adding Comments

One of the best ways to improve engagement with your site is by adding comments. Of course, whether or not comments are a good idea is totally based on the type of visitors to your site, but if you have a (generally!) good audience, then allowing them to comment can be an incredible way to increase traffic.

Multiple different services exist now to support adding comments to a site, whether static or dynamic. The most common options are:

- Disqus (*https://disqus.com*)
- Livefyre (*http://web.livefyre.com*)
- Facebook Comments (*https://developers.facebook.com/docs/plugins/comments*)

The most popular and easiest to test is Disqus, so let's see what's involved in using it.

Working with Disqus

The first thing you'll need to do is create an account (*https://disqus.com/profile/signup/*). After you sign up, you'll be prompted to select what you want to do: just write comments on existing sites or add comments to your site. See Figure 5-23.

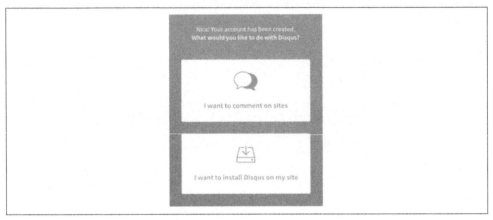

Figure 5-23. The Disqus signup process

Obviously, select the option for adding comments to your site. Next you'll be prompted to provide a name and category for your site, shown in Figure 5-24. Enter whatever makes sense here.

Figure 5-24. Setting up your Disqus site

After a quick notice from Disqus, you'll be asked what platform you're using. If you scroll to the bottom, you'll see an option for Universal Code (Figure 5-25); that's the one you want.

Figure 5-25. This is the option you're looking for

On the next screen, shown in Figure 5-26, you'll be given a script that you can copy and paste. There are other things you can tweak here (like configuration variables and CSS), but for now, simply copy that code.

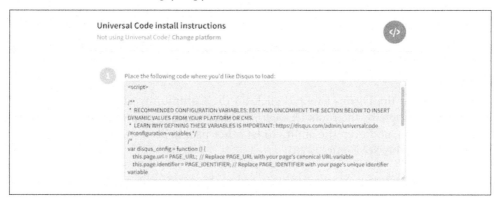

Figure 5-26. The code to add Disqus to your site

Create any HTML file you want, or use the file from the GitHub repo (*ch5/comments/ disqus1.html*) and copy in the Disqus code. Figure 5-27 shows how it looks out of the box running on a local web server.

Figure 5-27. Comments for the test page

You can now start adding comments. If you use the code from the GitHub repo and do *not* change the code, you'll see the comments I added while testing and comments from anyone else reading the book.

By default, Disqus uses the URL of the file to create a *thread*, or a unique set of comments. You can use the same code in another file and comments there will be different from the first file. You can see an example of this in *ch5/comments/disqus2.html* (*http://bit.ly/2lIPxfj*). The code is the same (except for the header), but the comments will be unique.

If you return to the Disqus site and click on the Community tab in the header, you can see an example of the tools Disqus provides. There are options for moderation, spam protection, and even the ability to let other people become moderators of comments on your site. See Figure 5-28.

Figure 5-28. The Disqus admin

You also get basic reporting options, but don't expect to see much immediately. I'm using Disqus for my blog (*https://www.raymondcamden.com*), so Figure 5-29 shows a screenshot from my site's dashboard:

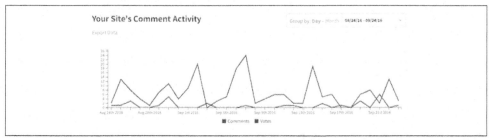

Figure 5-29. A chart showing comment activity on my blog

Adding Comments to The Cat Blog

In Chapter 3, you learned how to use Jekyll to build a simple blog. Now let's update the blog to use Disqus comments. In the GitHub repository for this book, you'll find a new version of the blog in *ch5/comments/catblog (http://bit.ly/2l4A31y)*. Jekyll's template files are found in the _layouts folder. If you open *post.html*, you'll see that the Disqus code used earlier has been copied and pasted into the layout. The exact position was kind of arbitrary. I placed it over the pagination HTML, but it could really go anywhere. Also, you don't need to restrict comments to blog posts only. If the blog also has an About page or other random pages, you can add commenting there as well.

And again—that's it! As Figure 5-30 shows, once added to the posts layout, every blog post will now have comments!

Figure 5-30. The Cat Blog—now with comments!

Adding Search

For a small static site like Camden Grounds, a user can browse the entire site in minutes. For larger sites, like a blog, it would be nearly impossible to do so. This is where having a search engine can be incredibly helpful. While a few options exist for adding search to a static site, the best option (at least in this author's opinion) is to use the undisputed king of search, Google.

Google provides a search called the Custom Search Engine (CSE). This service lets you create an embed that will use the power of Google's search index against a specific domain (or domains). This means you provide a Google-powered search for *only* your site's content, and nothing more. Let's take a look at how this is done.

Creating a Custom Search Engine

To begin, open your browser to *https://cse.google.com/cse* and log in with your Google account. (Of course Google requires that.) You can then click the big obvious blue button "Create a custom search engine" to begin.

In the simplest form, a CSE consists of a site to search and a name, as shown in Figure 5-31.

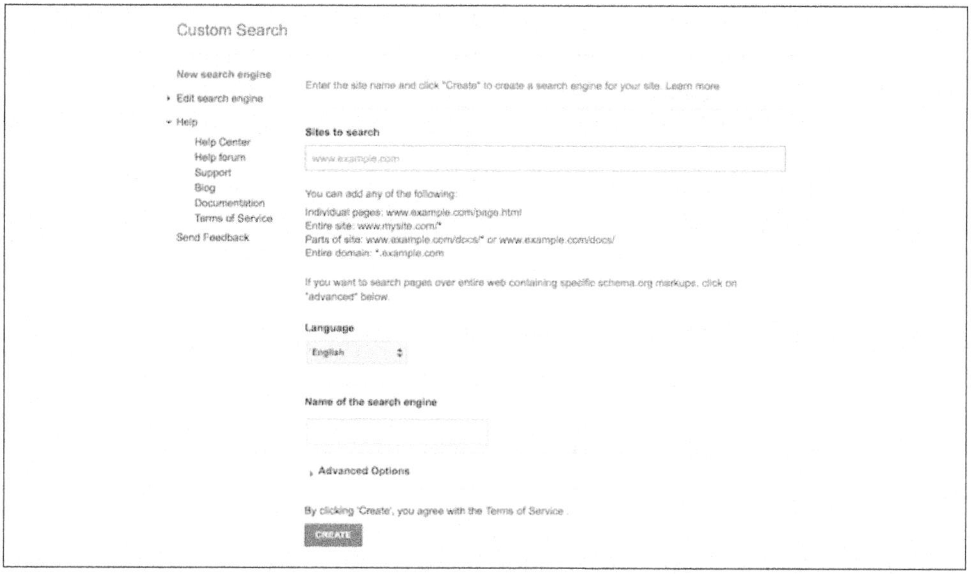

Figure 5-31. Creating a new custom search engine

In case it isn't obvious, Google wants a *live* URL for an existing site. You can certainly use a domain that isn't live yet, but Google won't be able to index it obviously. This also means that if you are just now launching your static site, the search engine won't actually be able to return anything yet. That could make testing a bit difficult at first. But once your site is deployed, Google will index it rather quickly. You can enter any value you want here; in order to get some content to show up immediately, enter the domain for my blog, raymondcamden.com. As the help text describes, you want to follow the domain with /* to signify that you want to search everything under the domain. Finally, for the name of the search engine, enter anything appropriate. For now we'll use Static Site Test. Hit the Create button and you're good to go, as shown in Figure 5-32.

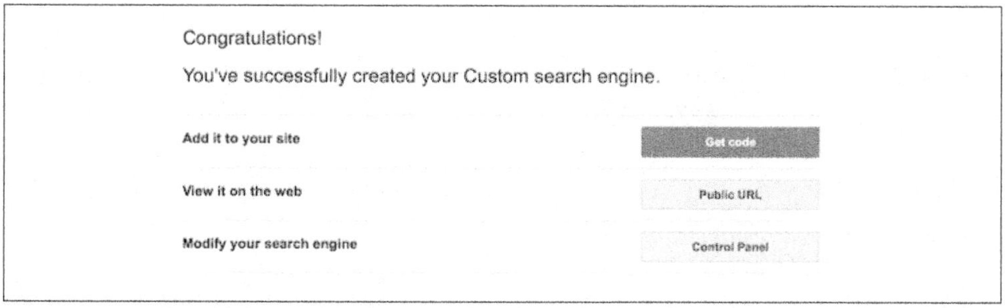

Figure 5-32. You've built the custom search engine

There are quite a few options that customize how the CSE works, but go ahead and just click the button to get the code. Take that code and drop it in any simple HTML page. If you've downloaded the code for this book, you'll find an example in *ch5/search/test.html* (*http://bit.ly/2lCY9nf*). By default, the embed provides both the search field and submit button. It takes the full width of the enclosing content, which means if you *don't* use CSS to restrict it, it will take up the entire width of the window. See Figure 5-33 for the result.

Figure 5-33. The embed in action!

You can go ahead and type something to test the search. If you're using the version from the GitHub repo or my URL for the search engine, try searching for "star wars" (Figure 5-34).

Figure 5-34. Search results from the CSE

You'll notice a few things right away. Yes, there are ads on top, and no, you can't get rid of them unless you upgrade to a paid version of the CSE. In the screenshot in Figure 5-34 the ads take up a *lot* of the space available, but keep in mind the window used for the figure was shrunk quite a bit. On a typical web page (which you'll see an example of pretty soon) it won't be as overwhelming. Next, notice how Google creates a floating-window effect for the results. And if you click one of the results, it opens in a new tab. All of that can be pretty annoying (though if you like that behavior, great!), but luckily you can change it pretty easily.

Back on the Google Custom Search Engine page, use the menu on the left and select "Look and feel". Under the Layout tab, you can see multiple different options to render the result. Clicking Full width will get rid of the overlay. Be sure to click the Save button, go back to Setup, and click Get code to get an updated version of the code. Reload your test page and you can see the change (Figure 5-35).

Figure 5-35. Nicer search results

Getting rid of the new window on search is a bit more of a pain. Unfortunately there is no simple toggle in the CSE settings. There is one CSE doc (*https://develop ers.google.com/custom-search/docs/element*) on customizing search results, which describes multiple arguments that you can add to the embed. Most services that give you embed code typically don't want you mucking with the code itself. They give it to you, you copy and paste it, and that's the end of it. But Google's CSE encourages you to modify the embed to fit your needs. This is the HTML portion of the embed as it comes, by default, from your new CSE:

```
<gcse:search></gcse:search>
```

The docs Google provides describe an option, linkTarget, that defaults to _blank. That's the issue right there. Edit the <gcse:search> tag to change this to _parent (you can find this in *test2.html*):

```
<gcse:search linkTarget="_parent"></gcse:search>
```

Now when you search and click results, it will act like most search engines. If you return to the dashboard, you'll find numerous other layout options to let you customize much more of the display of the results.

Adding a Custom Search Engine to a Real Site

In the previous sections of this chapter, we demonstrated adding dynamic aspects back to sites by using earlier examples from the book. For this final example, we'll use a site that's actually deployed live now: *https://raymondcamden.com*.

My site uses Hugo (covered in Chapter 4) as a static site generator. Currently, my blog has over 5,500 entries, making a good search engine a requirement. I created my CSE much as described in the previous section (changing the layout results to get rid of the overlay and using the `linkTarget` attribute) and then added it to a new page, *search.html*.

```
+++
title = "Search"
+++

<div>
<script>
(function() {
var cx = '013262903309526573707:i2otogiya2g';
var gcse = document.createElement('script');
gcse.type = 'text/javascript';
gcse.async = true;
gcse.src = (document.location.protocol == 'https:' ? 'https:' : 'http:') +
'//cse.google.com/cse.js?cx=' + cx;
var s = document.getElementsByTagName('script')[0];
s.parentNode.insertBefore(gcse, s);
})();
</script>
<gcse:search linktarget="_parent"></gcse:search>
</div>
```

The first thing to note is that the embed is surrounded by a simple empty `div` tag. Why? Markdown tried to render parts of the `gcse` tag and broke the embed. If the code is wrapped in a `div`, Markdown will ignore the content inside.

One more small tweak was needed to integrate the CSE into my site. On the top right corner of my blog is a search field. This form submits to the search page. In order for the CSE to "pick up" on the user input, I needed to name my search field "q". Here is the form:

```
<form action="{{ .Site.BaseURL}}search/"
  method="get" accept-charset="UTF-8" class="search-form">
    <input type="search" name="q" results="0" class="search-form-input"
    placeholder="{{with .Site.Data.l10n.search.placeholder}}{{.}}{{end}}">
    <button type="submit" class="search-form-submit"></button>
</form>
```

If you don't want to use the name "q" for any reason, you can also tell the CSE to use another field. As described in the documentation described earlier (*http://bit.ly/ 2ljry5x*), if you add `queryParameterName="something"` to the `gcse` tag, you can tell the embed to look for a value in another field name. The choice is yours.

Even More Options

We've only scratched the surface in terms of the types of services you can add to your static site. Here are a few more examples to consider:

- Google isn't the only option for search. You can even use completely client-side solutions like lunr.js (*http://lunrjs.com/*). I believe solutions like this are fundamentally dangerous as your content scales, but if you're sure about the size—and *potential* size—of your site, it may be an acceptable solution.
- If your organization has events, you may consider using a service like Eventbrite (*https://www.eventbrite.com/*). Eventbrite can help you manage events and track attendees, and it also lets you embed your events on your site.
- Another option for events is Google Calendar (*https://www.google.com/calendar*). Google Calendar has embed options as well, although in my experience the UI customization was a bit limited.
- If you remember that static site generators let you create non-HTML files too (like XML and JSON files), you could integrate with a plugin like FullCalendar (*https://fullcalendar.io/*). This jQuery plugin creates a nice interactive calendar that can integrate with a local data file (and Google Calendar too!). It gives you great control over the look and feel of how the calendar is used on the site.
- The "nuclear" option may be something like Firebase (*https://fire base.google.com/*). This is a complete "data as a service" provider where anything at all can be stored. It provides a JavaScript client that can be used within a static site. This feels a bit like overkill to me, but it's an option to consider nonetheless.

Finally, keep in mind that any external service creates a dependency that is out of your control. You have to consider what will happen if that remote service goes down. How do you contact them to report an outage? How quickly do they respond? Also, some people automatically block certain embeds, like Disqus. Are you okay with that? These are all things you need to consider before employing these services.

## CHAPTER 6

Adding a CMS

Brian Rinaldi

Although using static site generators for both large- and small-scale sites has been gaining in acceptance among developers, the experience for content contributors is still generally suboptimal. This is especially true for anyone who is used to editing content using WYSIWYG editing tools in popular blog engines like WordPress and other content management systems. Transitioning from using these content editors to writing Markdown files in a text editor is probably a deal breaker for many companies. Solving this problem can often be more difficult than solving the technology problem, as Stefan Baumgartner describes in his article *Using A Static Site Generator At Scale: Lessons Learned* (*http://bit.ly/2ljrMJV*):

> The biggest challenge in our journey to static sites was getting content editors to work with the new technology stack. You have to be hard as nails if you are willing to leave the comforts of your WYSIWYG editor—you know, those same comforts that drive web developers insane.

Stefan's solution was to build a WYSIWYG editor for their less technical contributors, but this isn't a viable option for every project or team.

Beyond the difficulties of editing content, publishing that content is a non-trivial matter for the average nontechnical content contributor. Depending on the setup, they either have to learn to test, build, and FTP or how to commit and sync using something like GitHub to post their content. This can seem overwhelming to someone with a nontechnical background who was used to just typing and hitting "publish."

The good news is that a number of tools have arisen in recent years to make the process of creating and editing static sites easier for less technical users. Most of these are not free, but they do offer a range of features beyond a WYSIWYG content tool. In this chapter, we'll look at a handful of these, including CloudCannon (*http://cloudcan*

non.com/), Netlify CMS (*https://github.com/netlify/netlify-cms*), and Jekyll Admin (*https://github.com/jekyll/jekyll-admin*).

CloudCannon

CloudCannon (*http://cloudcannon.com/*) is a cloud-based CMS specifically for Jekyll sites. Though you can try it for free, it is a commercial product that offers various plans depending on your site's specific needs. CloudCannon is a hosted service, which means that it won't work if your business requires that your site be on-premise. But because it is a hosted service, it offers some additional benefits such as automatic optimizations including GZIP, minification, and loading assets from a CDN (*https:// en.wikipedia.org/wiki/Content_delivery_network*).

Another important consideration is that CloudCannon supports a limited set of Jekyll versions—currently 2.4.0 by default, and 2.5.3 and 3.0.3 via configuration settings. This shouldn't be an issue for a greenfield project (*https://en.wikipedia.org/wiki/Green field_project*) but could come into play if you are transitioning an existing Jekyll codebase. In addition, while CloudCannon does support Jekyll extensions, the feature is still in private beta as of this writing.

For full feature support and usage details, refer to CloudCannon's documentation (*https://docs.cloudcannon.com*).

Creating a Site on CloudCannon

In order to create a site on CloudCannon, you need to sign up for an account. There's a free 30-day trial, after which point it will revert to a free account that has strict limitations on features and adds a splash page to your site.

Once you have an account and are logged in, click Create Site, as shown in Figure 6-1.

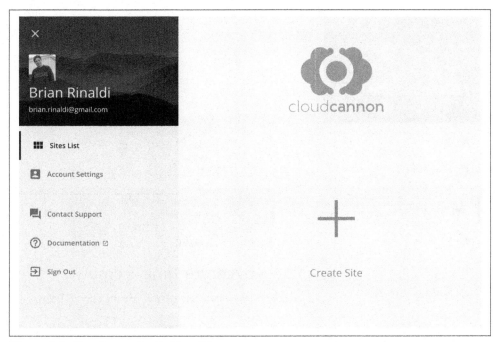

Figure 6-1. Creating a site in CloudCannon

You'll be prompted to give your site a name. For this tutorial, we'll use a sample from a series I created for various static site engines (*https://github.com/remotesynth/Static-Site-Samples*). Obviously, in this case, we'll use the Jekyll version (*http://bit.ly/2kVHDeg*). To make this process easier, I've placed a zip of the sample files in the *ch6* folder of the GitHub repository for this book. Download it (*http://bit.ly/2liVqP7*) and unzip it. (Note that I made some minor tweaks to the original source code to optimize it for some of CloudCannon's features.)

Since all of these samples are from an Adventure Time! (*http://www.imdb.com/title/tt1305826/*) fan site, let's name the site Adventure Time (Figure 6-2).

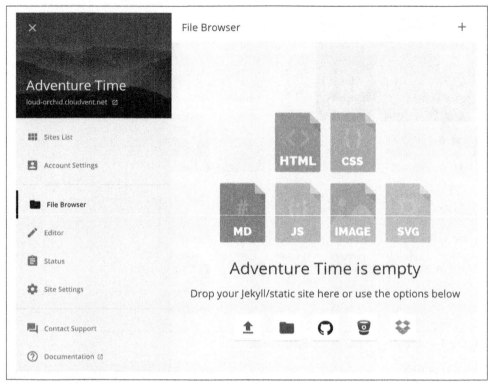

Figure 6-2. A newly created site on CloudCannon

One of the great things about CloudCannon is that it gives you a lot of options for pushing your Jekyll site onto its system. You can upload files individually, upload the contents of entire folders, connect to a GitHub or BitBucket repository, or even pull files from DropBox.

To make things easy, for this example we'll use the folder option. Click the folder icon and select the folder containing the unzipped sample you downloaded earlier. After the upload is complete, your files should look like those in Figure 6-3.

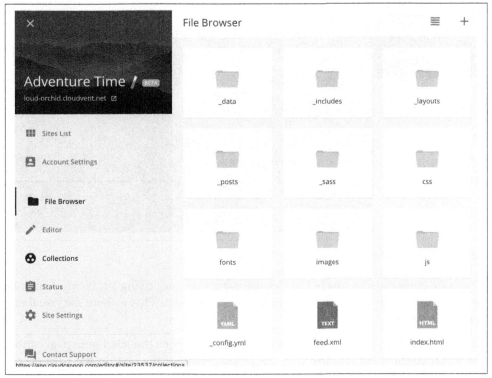

Figure 6-3. Uploaded source files on CloudCannon

Editing a Site on CloudCannon

Now that we've uploaded the files, let's look at some of CloudCannon's editing options.

The first option allows you to edit any file in a web-based code editor (Figure 6-4) by clicking on it in the file browser.

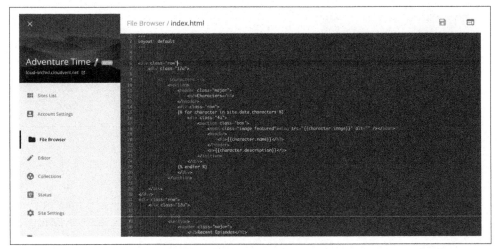

Figure 6-4. The CloudCannon code editor

The code editor works nicely but doesn't solve our underlying problem of making content easier to create and edit for nontechnical authors. That's where the visual editor comes into play.

Click the Editor option in the lefthand menu. This opens the site home page within the visual editor interface. You may notice that some of the text on the page is outlined in yellow (Figure 6-5). These areas can be directly edited by the user.

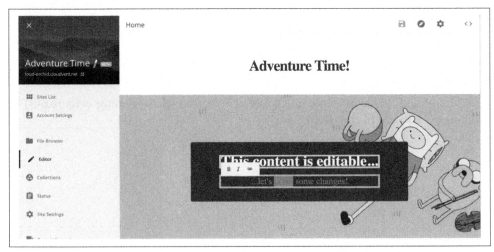

Figure 6-5. The outlined content can be edited and formatted by the end user

Let's go ahead and click on the top editable item that reads "This content is editable..." You should be able to edit the text and apply some basic formatting (e.g., bold, italics, add links). In this case, formatting options are limited because we are editing a text element rather than a block element.

You can replace the text with whatever you like. I replaced the top with "Explore the Land of Ooo..." and the bottom with "...and its many kingdoms!"

So, how is editing text within the layout enabled? You simply add a `class=editable` to the tag in the template. In this case, I added it to the `h2` and `p` tags in the header, as you can see here:

```
<header>
    <h2 class="editable">This content is editable...</h2>
    <p class="editable">...let's make some changes!</p>
</header>
```

However, we can edit more than just plain text. Scroll down to the bottom of the home page in the editor and you should see an editable image and formatted text area within the footer.

Click on the image to access the image editing options, shown in Figure 6-6.

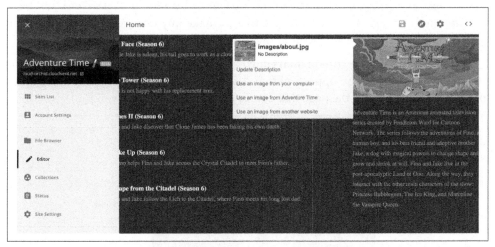

Figure 6-6. Editing an image in the CloudCannon visual editor

Clicking on the formatted text area gives you more formatting options than the plain-text area (see Figure 6-7).

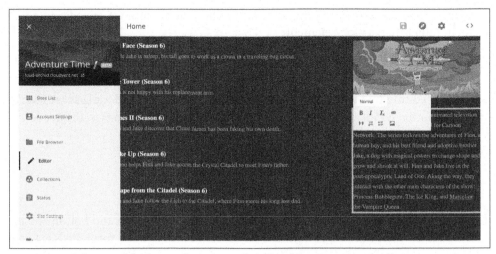

Figure 6-7. Editing a block text element in the CloudCannon visual editor

The images and text were also made editable simply by adding `class="editable"` to the `img` and `div` tags, respectively. Feel free to make any changes you like and then save them by clicking the save icon in the upper righthand corner of the editor.

Lastly, let's look at how to edit Markdown content in CloudCannon. Click on the "toggle pages" icon in the upper righthand corner of the editor (it looks like a compass). See Figure 6-8 for the page that comes up after doing so.

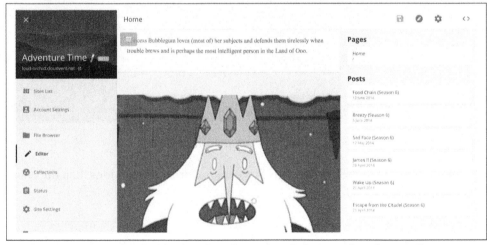

Figure 6-8. Pages and posts listed in the editor after clicking on "toggle pages"

Next, let's choose the first post, "Food Chain (Season 6)." This opens the page in the visual editor (you may want to toggle off the pages menu at this point for a better view). Now you can see the page content within the editor and change any of the editable elements on the page (i.e., the image and formatted text in the footer). However, what we'd like to do is edit the actual contents of the post.

To do this, click the "switch to content editor" icon in the upper righthand corner of the visual editor (it looks like a pencil). This opens the contents of the post in the content editor, where you can edit the body using visual formatting tools (much like those from the formatted text area above). This means your user doesn't need to know or understand Markdown to edit or create a page.

You might notice that you can't edit the title of the page in the editor. You'll have to use the CloudCannon content editor for this; it allows you to edit any of the settings for the page or post (these are the metadata items placed in the YAML front matter on Jekyll posts and pages).

Click the "toggle settings" icon on the upper righthand corner of the page (it looks like a gear). This opens the settings editor, shown in Figure 6-9.

Figure 6-9. Editing post content and settings in the CloudCannon content editor

The editor allows you to edit standard metadata properties like title and date, as well as custom properties like the shortdesc and banner properties for our sample site.

Where to Go from Here

I've only touched on the basics of CloudCannon. Still, as you can see, it provides a lot of functionality that makes it easier for users who aren't comfortable editing HTML, Liquid, YAML, and Markdown to make changes and maintain the site content. To learn more about the editors or hosting, check out the CloudCannon site (*http://cloud cannon.com/*) or documentation (*https://docs.cloudcannon.com/*).

Netlify CMS

The Netlify CMS (*https://github.com/netlify/netlify-cms*) is not a hosted service like CloudCannon, but rather a free and open source CMS-style admin that you can add to your static site project. The project is created and maintained by Netlify (*https://www.netlify.com/*). Netlify does offer a popular service for continuous deployment and hosting of static sites, but it's not required to use the CMS project.

In addition to being free, the Netlify CMS has the benefit of not being exclusively tied to Jekyll. Because it only offers a backend to the content and data, it can, in theory, work with any static site generator. In fact, the project offers templates to work with Jekyll, Roots (*http://roots.cx/*), Hexo (*https://hexo.io/*), and Pelican (*http://blog.getpelican.com/*).

Versions of Netlify CMS

As of this writing, the original version of Netlify CMS, which was built using the Ember framework, was the most complete version. However, the tool is currently being rebuilt using the React framework, which will eventually replace the existing Ember version of the tool. This tutorial uses the Ember version.

Setting Up the Netlify CMS

The two solutions we've explored so far have focused specifically on Jekyll. Let's try setting up the Netlify CMS for a static site using the Hexo static site generator (*https://hexo.io/*).

We'll start by getting a basic Hexo site running. I've placed a zip of the sample files in the *ch6* folder (*http://bit.ly/2miajiC*) of the GitHub, or you can download the zip file here (*http://bit.ly/2m8pAmF*). Unzip it wherever you want to work on your project.

Sample Template

The example here is based upon the Hexo template (*https://github.com/netlify-templates/hexo-cms-example*) provided as part of the Netlify CMS, which, in turn, was based on my static site samples project (*https://github.com/remotesynth/Static-Site-Samples*). The project includes some minor modifications to the original source to allow the tool to edit character data.

Hexo is a JavaScript-based generator that runs on Node.js. If you don't already have Node and npm installed, download and install it now (*https://nodejs.org/en/*). In addition, to make Netlify CMS run locally, you need to have Git installed (*https://git-scm.com/*).

Once Node and Git are installed, let's start by getting our Hexo site running. Open a terminal or command prompt in the folder that contains the sample site. Once there, install Hexo and all of the necessary dependencies by simply doing an `npm install` via the command line.

Since we're installing things, there's one more piece that isn't necessary for Hexo but will be necessary to run the Netlify CMS—the Netlify Git API (*https://github.com/netlify/netlify-git-api*). It turns your local Git repository into a REST API that the Netlify CMS web application can call to do things like modify the content or add user access.

To install it, first grab the appropriate version for your operating system (*https://github.com/netlify/netlify-git-api/releases*). Next, unzip the file, making sure to note where you place the unzipped file (for instance, on Windows, you might simply place the file in a folder named *C://netlify-git-api* or on a Mac OS in */Applications/netlify-git-api*. The final step is to add the folder to your path variable (*http://bit.ly/14smsVa*). You can find instructions for Windows (*http://bit.ly/2l4wkRy*) or for Mac (*http://bit.ly/2ljqe2A*). If you have a terminal or command prompt window open already, you'll need to close and reopen it for it to see changes to the path.

If you've done everything properly, you should be able to call `netlify-git-api` from the command line without error. For example, you can see in Figure 6-10 that the folder was added to my `$PATH` on my Mac, as well as the results of calling the command.

```
MCWFHBRRINALD:hexosite brinaldi$ echo $PATH
/usr/local/bin:/usr/local/bin:/usr/bin:/bin:/usr/sbin:/sbin:/Applications/netlify-git-api
MCWFHBRRINALD:hexosite brinaldi$ netlify-git-api
usage: netlify-git-api [<flags>] <command> [<args> ...]

Get a REST API for a Git repository

Flags:
  --help              Show help (also see --help-long and --help-man).
  --db=".users.yml"   File path to the user db

Commands:
  help [<command>...]
    Show help.

  serve [<flags>]
    Start a local Git API server

  users list
    List all users

  users add [<flags>]
    Add a new user

  users del [<email>]
    Remove a user


MCWFHBRRINALD:hexosite brinaldi$ ▌
```

Figure 6-10. The netlify-git-api added to the $PATH on Mac and the results of calling the command

If everything has finished installing, enter the following command to start the local Hexo server:

```
hexo serve -o
```

The -o option tells Hexo to open the page in your default browser automatically. You should see a version of the "Adventure Time!" fan page that I use as part of my static site samples project (*https://github.com/remotesynth/Static-Site-Samples*).

The sample already includes the Netlify CMS admin template based upon the Hexo template (*https://github.com/netlify-templates/hexo-cms-example*) they provide. However, it is important to understand how it was set up if you intend to build your own or modify the existing template to suit your needs.

Finally, in a separate terminal or command prompt tab or window, let's go ahead and set up and start the Netlify Git API so that we can explore the CMS admin. First things first, you'll need to make sure you add the project to a local Git repository. Assuming that your command prompt is already open at the project's location, type the following commands:

```
git init
git add .
git commit -m "First commit"
```

Now that we have a Git repository to work against, we can add a user to it via the Netlify Git API.

```
netlify-git-api users add
```

This command will start a series of prompts asking for the user's information. After it is complete, start the Netlify Git API by entering the command **netlify-git-api serve**.

Exploring the Netlify CMS configuration

Within the sample project, open the file */source/admin/index.ejs* (EJS is one of the default templating languages used by Hexo). This file is based on the default HTML and configuration from the Netlify CMS documentation (*https://github.com/netlify/netlify-cms#installing*). The key changes are in the configuration portion, which you can see in Example 6-1:

Example 6-1. Configuration portion of EJS file

```
backend:
  name: netlify-api
  url: http://localhost:8080

media_folder: "source/assets/images" # Folder where user uploaded
                                      # files should go
public_folder: "source"

collections: # A list of collections the CMS should be able to edit
  - name: "posts" # Used in routes, ie.: /admin/collections/:slug/edit
    label: "Post" # Used in the UI, ie.: "New Post"
    folder: "source/_posts" # The path to the folder where the
                            # documents are stored
    sort: "date:desc"
    create: true # Allow users to create new documents in this collection
    fields: # The fields each document in this collection have
      - {label: "Title", name: "title", widget: "string", tagname: "h1"}
      - {label: "Banner", name: "banner", widget: "image",
         class: "image featured"}
      - {label: "Short Description", name: "shortdesc", widget: "string"}
      - {label: "Body", name: "body", widget: "markdown"}
    meta: # Meta data fields. Just like fields, but without any preview element
      - {label: "Publish Date", name: "date", widget: "datetime"}
      - {label: "Categories", name: "categories", widget: "string"}
      - {label: "Layout", name: "layout", widget: "hidden", default: "post"}
  - name: "data"
    label: "Data"
    files:
      - name: "characters"
        label: "Characters"
        file: "source/_data/characters.yml"
```

```
fields:
  - label: "Characters"
    name: "list"
    widget: "list"
    fields:
      - {label: "Name", name: "name", widget: "string"}
      - {label: "Image", name: "image", widget: "image",
          media_folder: "assets/images"}
      - {label: "Description", name: "description", widget: "string"}
```

We'll explore the backend a bit more in a moment, but first let's explore the pieces of this configuration.

The `backend` property is essentially our REST API, which in this case is the Netlify Git API that we set up earlier.

The `media_folder` designates where uploaded files, such as images for posts or pages, will be placed. The `public_folder` tells the CMS the path to the source files so that the path to assets won't include it. For example, the `media_folder` here is `/source/assets/images`, but the path in the generated site will only be `/assets/images`.

The `collections` property defines the different types of content that the CMS can edit. In the case of our example site, the user will be able to add/edit posts as well as character data. In order for this to work, the CMS needs to understand a little bit about the data these contain. The `fields` and `meta` properties under each define the data as well as the type of widget that will be used in the UI to edit it. The primary difference between them is that `fields` are generally elements of the page that will be displayed in the visual editor (i.e., they will be displayed in some manner on the page as well). Meanwhile, `meta` are metadata elements that are not typically displayed and can be edited in the "settings" for each entry.

The benefit of this approach to defining the data is that we can define custom properties. For example, our posts contain properties like a "short description" (`shortdesc`) and "banner," which are not part of a default Hexo post. It also means that we can allow users to edit data in YAML files, such as our site's character data. The one special thing to notice about the data structure for our characters is that we can define `fields` within `fields`, meaning we can manage even fairly complex data files.

However, this flexibility means that we also need to tell the CMS how to preview the output of our posts and data. See Example 6-2. This is also defined in *index.ejs*, just below the configuration code in Example 6-1.

Example 6-2. Previewing post and data outputs

```
<script type="text/x-handlebars" data-template-name='cms/preview/posts'>
    <div id="main-wrapper">
        <div class="container">
            <!--Content-->
            <article class="box post">
                {{#if entry.banner }}
                {{cms-preview field='banner'}}
                {{/if}}
                <header>
                    <h2>{{ entry.title }}</h2>
                    <p>{{ entry.shortdesc}}</p>
                </header>
                {{cms-preview field='body'}}
            </article>
        </div>
    </div>
</script>


<script type="text/x-handlebars" data-template-name='cms/preview/characters'>
    <div id="main-wrapper">
        <div class="container">
            {{#cms-preview field="list" as |character| }}
              <section class="box">
                  <span class="image featured">
                    {{cms-preview field="image" from=character}}
                      </span>
                  <header>
                      <h3>{{character.name}}</h3>
                  </header>
                  <p>{{character.description}}</p>
              </section>
            {{/cms-preview}}
        </div>
    </div>
</script>
```

This file defines Handlebars (*http://handlebarsjs.com/*) templates that tell the CMS how to display the output of our data. The first `script` block defines this for posts and the second for character data. This allows us not only to include our custom properties (like the short description), but also to match the preview to the actual page display as closely as possible.

Taking the Netlify CMS for a test run

Now that we've explored how to install and configure the Netlify CMS, let's quickly look at how it works for a user editing the content. Go to *http://localhost:4000/admin*

in your browser (remember that your local Hexo server should be running on port 4000 by default).

We're first prompted to log in (Figure 6-11). We will use the user information that we created earlier when configuring the Netlify Git API.

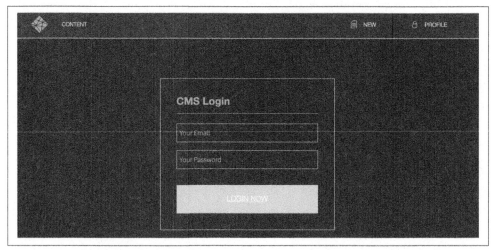

Figure 6-11. The login form for the Netlify CMS admin

After we log in, we are presented with a list of the existing posts on the site (Figure 6-12).

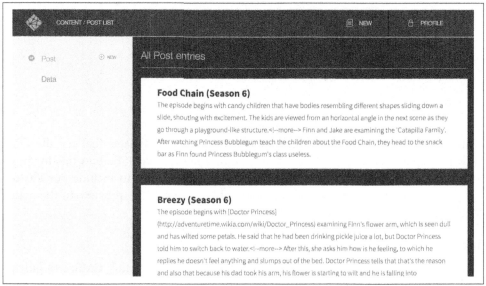

Figure 6-12. All post entries in the Netlify CMS from our sample site

Clicking on a post opens the visual editor (Figure 6-13). Feel free to try it out and change some of the post's contents. Be sure to click the Settings button in the lower righthand corner to see how to edit the post's metadata. If you make any changes, click Save to save them.

Figure 6-13. Editing a post using the Netlify CMS visual editor

To get back to the admin home, click the Content link at the upper lefthand corner of the page. Next click on Data in the menu on the left. This should bring up a list of the types of data that we can edit, which right now is only the characters (Figure 6-14).

Figure 6-14. The available data types to edit via the Netlify CMS

Click on Characters. This opens a visual editor for character data (Figure 6-15). Feel free to add or edit entries in our characters.

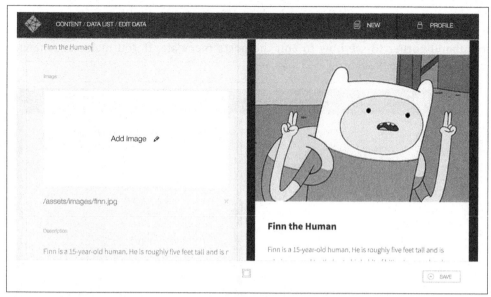

Figure 6-15. Editing character data via the Netlify CMS admin

Because we're editing static files on the filesystem, any changes we save should show up immediately in our site preview (you might need to refresh the browser to see them).

Where to Go from Here

Obviously, the Netlify CMS takes a decent amount of set up and configuration to get going, but it also offers a ton of flexibility. In this case, we are editing the key content elements of our site via an easy-to-use visual editor using the static site generator of our choice—in this case, Hexo. For anyone keen on using a particular static site generator, especially if they plan to customize it, this can be an ideal option for adding a CMS. If you would like to learn more about the Netlify CMS, check out the full documentation on GitHub (*https://github.com/netlify/netlify-cms*).

Jekyll Admin

Jekyll Admin (*https://github.com/jekyll/jekyll-admin*) is an extremely recent development, having only been released publicly in August of 2016 (literally as I was writing this chapter). It isn't quite as full-featured as some of the other offerings we've looked at so far, but it has a couple of key things going for it.

First, it is the only officially supported CMS-like tool from any of the static site generator projects (at least that I am aware of). Not only that, but it is from the most popular and most widely supported static site generator available. (This probably also means that it sets an example other projects are likely to follow.)

Second, it is extremely easy to set up, while requiring no monthly subscription and no special configuration. Basically, if you have a Jekyll site, you can simply add the admin on and start adding and editing content using its graphical interface.

In my opinion, this kind of freely available and officially supported solution could potentially have a big impact on the adoption not just of Jekyll but of static site generators as a solution in general. That being said, the project is still very young, so it may not yet match the typical expectations of someone coming from a more traditional CMS solution. Let's take a look.

Setting Up Jekyll Admin

As I mentioned already, the setup and installation are incredibly simple. Let's walk through adding it to the Jekyll version of the sample site (*http://bit.ly/2kVHDeg*) from my static site samples GitHub repository (*https://github.com/remotesynth/Static-Site-Samples*). To make things a little easier, you can simply download a zip of the Jekyll site files (*http://bit.ly/2lrytYC*). Unzip them wherever you'd like to work on your project.

Assuming Jekyll is already installed (from earlier chapters in this book), the next thing we need to do is install Jekyll Admin. The easiest way is via RubyGems (*https://rubygems.org/*).

```
gem install jekyll-admin
```

Inside the project files, open up `_config.yml` and add the following line:

```
gems: [jekyll-admin]
```

That's it! Now just open the terminal or command prompt at the project folder and start Jekyll as you normally would.

```
jekyll serve
```

Jekyll Admin is up and running. You can access it by going to *http://localhost:4000/admin*.

Editing a Site in Jekyll Admin

Opening the site admin (shown in Figure 6-16) makes it apparent that Jekyll Admin assumes that if you have access to the admin, you are allowed to edit the entire site. This is an important consideration because one of the key features of Jekyll Admin is that it allows you to edit and, where applicable, create just about every aspect of the site from the configuration file, assets, pages, and posts.

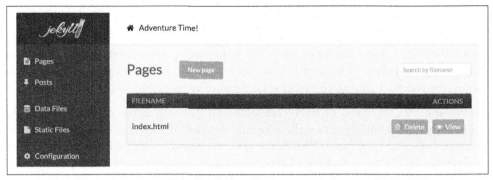

Figure 6-16. The main page of Jekyll Admin allows you to create and edit site pages

Creating or editing pages (as well as posts) assumes that you are working in Markdown. So, while you can edit *index.html*, the formatting shortcuts on the editor add Markdown-specific formatting.

Let's take a quick look at the editing features (Figure 6-17).

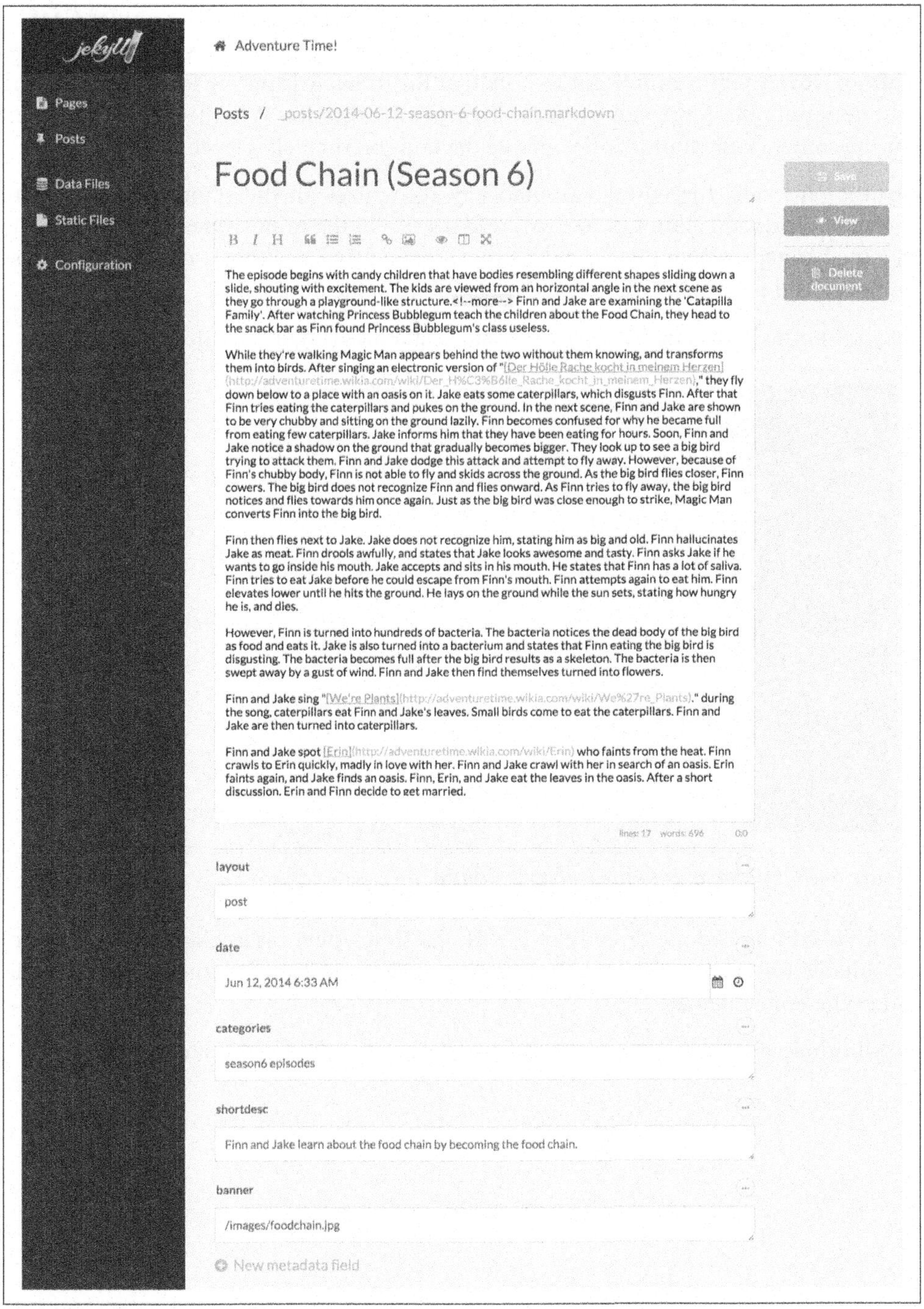

The episode begins with candy children that have bodies resembling different shapes sliding down a slide, shouting with excitement. The kids are viewed from an horizontal angle in the next scene as they go through a playground-like structure.<!--more--> Finn and Jake are examining the 'Catapilla Family'. After watching Princess Bubblegum teach the children about the Food Chain, they head to the snack bar as Finn found Princess Bubblegum's class useless.

While they're walking Magic Man appears behind the two without them knowing, and transforms them into birds. After singing an electronic version of "[Der Hölle Rache kocht in meinem Herzen](http://adventuretime.wikia.com/wiki/Der_H%C3%B6lle_Rache_kocht_in_meinem_Herzen)," they fly down below to a place with an oasis on it. Jake eats some caterpillars, which disgusts Finn. After that Finn tries eating the caterpillars and pukes on the ground. In the next scene, Finn and Jake are shown to be very chubby and sitting on the ground lazily. Finn becomes confused for why he became full from eating few caterpillars. Jake informs him that they have been eating for hours. Soon, Finn and Jake notice a shadow on the ground that gradually becomes bigger. They look up to see a big bird trying to attack them. Finn and Jake dodge this attack and attempt to fly away. However, because of Finn's chubby body, Finn is not able to fly and skids across the ground. As the big bird flies closer, Finn cowers. The big bird does not recognize Finn and flies onward. As Finn tries to fly away, the big bird notices and flies towards him once again. Just as the big bird was close enough to strike, Magic Man converts Finn into the big bird.

Finn then flies next to Jake. Jake does not recognize him, stating him as big and old. Finn hallucinates Jake as meat. Finn drools awfully, and states that Jake looks awesome and tasty. Finn asks Jake if he wants to go inside his mouth. Jake accepts and sits in his mouth. He states that Finn has a lot of saliva. Finn tries to eat Jake before he could escape from Finn's mouth. Finn attempts again to eat him. Finn elevates lower until he hits the ground. He lays on the ground while the sun sets, stating how hungry he is, and dies.

However, Finn is turned into hundreds of bacteria. The bacteria notices the dead body of the big bird as food and eats it. Jake is also turned into a bacterium and states that Finn eating the big bird is disgusting. The bacteria becomes full after the big bird results as a skeleton. The bacteria is then swept away by a gust of wind. Finn and Jake then find themselves turned into flowers.

Finn and Jake sing "[We're Plants](http://adventuretime.wikia.com/wiki/We%27re_Plants)," during the song, caterpillars eat Finn and Jake's leaves. Small birds come to eat the caterpillars. Finn and Jake are then turned into caterpillars.

Finn and Jake spot [Erin](http://adventuretime.wikia.com/wiki/Erin) who faints from the heat. Finn crawls to Erin quickly, madly in love with her. Finn and Jake crawl with her in search of an oasis. Erin faints again, and Jake finds an oasis. Finn, Erin, and Jake eat the leaves in the oasis. After a short discussion. Erin and Finn decide to get married.

Figure 6-17. Editing a post in Jekyll Admin

The text editor is not the WYSIWYG style editor that is common in popular CMSes. Instead, you edit directly in Markdown, and can preview the output via a preview button. However, it is important to note that the preview is purely for text formatting and does not offer a preview of the content within the site. Whether this is sufficient for the content contributors on your site depends on their skill level.

On the plus side, the editor automatically recognizes all the standard and custom metadata fields and allows us to easily add more. On the minus side, editing metadata like the banner or layout is done via simple text editing, making it difficult to choose an image and potentially easy to make a typo the name of a layout.

Jekyll Admin also lets us edit any of the sites data files (Figure 6-18).

Figure 6-18. Editing a data file in Jekyll Admin

Data file editing is done directly in YAML via simple text input. Again, this may not be suitable for your nontechnical content contributors. The site configuration is edited in the same manner.

Jekyll Admin also makes it easy to add or delete static files for the site (Figure 6-19).

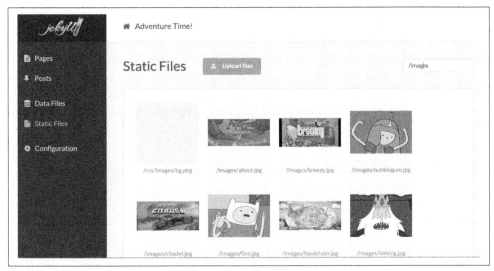

Figure 6-19. Viewing static site files in Jekyll Admin

Note that this view currently includes any static file on the site, including CSS files and JavaScript files as well as images and assets. Someone with less experience could easily delete the wrong file by mistake. Also, there is currently no way to specify where an upload should be placed (they all end up in the site root), making this far less useful for adding images to pages or posts.

Where to Go from Here

Jekyll Admin is extremely easy to install and configure, and allows you to add and edit pretty much any aspect of your site directly from within its visual editor. However, it has some limitations that might make it useful for only your nontechnical contributors. That being said, it is an extremely new project and I certainly expect many of these issues to be addressed as it matures.

To learn more about the project, check out its GitHub repository (*https://github.com/ jekyll/jekyll-admin*).

More Options

As static sites become more popular, a growing list of companies and projects are stepping in to add the CMS-like features that many users have come to expect when editing a site. Unfortunately, there is not enough space to cover them all here, but before we move on to the next chapter, I want to mention a couple of significant options.

Forestry.io

Forestry.io (*http://forestry.io/*) offers a service similar to CloudCannon but with some differentiating features such as support for both Jekyll and Hugo (*https://gohugo.io/*) as well as the ability to easily deploy to a large number of destinations including AWS, GitHub, and FTP. Editing a page or post allows you to easily modify standard or custom metadata attributes (and even choose the editor—for example, allowing you to edit the banner as an image but the description as text). See Figure 6-20.

Figure 6-20. Editing a post in the Forestry.io demo site

The editor is a Markdown editor (like Jekyll Admin) rather than a WYSIWYG editor (like CloudCannon), but it does have a shortcut that makes it easy to add images to a page or post, and the form also allows you to view an in-layout preview of the content. (On a side note, I love that so many of these tools use my Static Site Samples site for their demo apps.) Of course, you can also edit data and site menus using a simple visual editor.

Forestry.io is currently free for sites with up to 10 users without technical support. Paid plans are offered for more than 10 users or if you would like technical support.

Lektor

The final tool I want to mention is another very recent entry called Lektor (*https://www.getlektor.com/*). Lektor is a static site generator built in Python. What makes it different from other Python-based tools like Pelican (*http://blog.getpelican.com/*), for instance, is that it has both a built-in admin as well as an installable desktop application (currently Mac OS X only).

The Lektor desktop application (Figure 6-21) is designed to simplify running a local Lektor-based site that you already have on your computer, while also offering quick access to view and edit the site in a browser.

Figure 6-21. The Lektor desktop app running a sample site on Mac OS X

The admin for a Lektor site (Figure 6-22) is pretty basic in terms of content editing: content is Markdown edited within a simple text area. However, it has a number of built-in features for building out your site structure, uploading attachments, and even deploying the site from the admin.

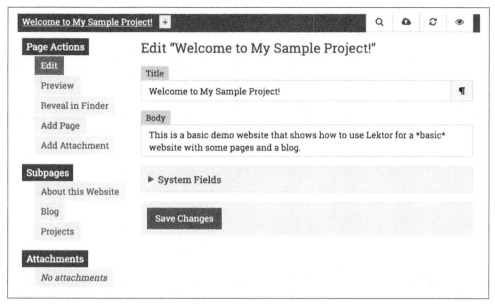

Figure 6-22. Editing a page in the Lektor site admin

As I mentioned, Lektor is also a relatively new project and it wouldn't be surprising to see it add more robust editing features into the admin or desktop tooling.

Headless CMS

One last option I want to mention is the concept of using a static site as the frontend to a *headless CMS* (*https://css-tricks.com/what-is-a-headless-cms/*). The term headless CMS is used because these services offer the backend user interface of a traditional CMS for adding and editing content, without the frontend (i.e., the website the content goes in). Instead, the service offers an API that you can connect to anything—a website, a native mobile app, or anything else that can consume this content.

In the case of a static site, rather than store your content as Markdown or YAML files on the filesystem, you store it in this CMS backend. Then you connect to the CMS backend via the API to generate your site.

A popular headless CMS service is Contentful (*https://www.contentful.com/*), which already offers official plugins for Jekyll (*https://www.contentful.com/ecosystem/jekyll/*) and Middleman (*https://www.contentful.com/ecosystem/middleman/*). There is also an unofficial Hugo tool for Contentful (*https://github.com/ArnoNuyts/contentful2hugo*). Another option is DatoCMS (*https://www.datocms.com/*), which offers prebuilt integration with the Jekyll, Middleman, Hugo, Metalsmith, Hexo, and Pelican static site generators.

The benefit of this option is that you are able to offer the CMS-style content editing that your authors prefer, and consume that content within your static site, but also consume it within any other type of application that can connect to the API.

## CHAPTER 7

Deployment

Raymond Camden

One of the biggest selling points of static sites is that their production requirements are essentially nil. But even with the minimal requirements for supporting a static site, there are still multiple options for developers to choose from.

In this chapter, we'll discuss the various ways you can take those simple, static files from your development machine and make them available to the world at large. Which you use depends entirely on your needs.

Plain Old Web Servers

Probably the simplest and most familiar solution is to make use of the same old web servers we've been using for the past 20 or so years. The two most popular options are the HTTP server from Apache (*http://httpd.apache.org/*) and IIS from Microsoft (*http://www.iis.net/*). Apache is available on multiple platforms, while IIS is only available on Windows.

In both cases, if you have the server set up, "deployment" is simply a matter of copying the output from your static site generator into the web root (or a relevant subdirectory) for your server.

It is likely that you don't want to manually copy files every time, so you could look into tools that make that process easier, like Grunt (*http://gruntjs.com/*) and Gulp (*http://gulpjs.com/*). Or you can simply use an old-school shell script or BAT file.

There's nothing special about this setup and nothing else really to say, and that's a good thing!

Cloud File Storage Providers

Most developers are probably aware of cloud services provided by Amazon, Google, Microsoft, and others, that provide basic file storage. The idea is that you can provision space and then load as many files as you would like. You don't have to worry about the size of the disk; you essentially treat it as an infinite hard drive to use as you see fit. (With costs, of course.)

What you may not know is that many of these services also provide a way to turn their file storage system into a simple web server. In this section, we'll take a look at how this is done with both Amazon's S3 service and Google's Cloud Storage service. Let's start with Amazon.

Hosting a Site on Amazon S3

Hosting with Amazon S3 requires you to have an AWS Account. You will need to provide a credit card during setup, but Amazon includes a large amount of disk space in their free tier. Obviously, you should double-check to ensure that the price is something you can afford, but in general, S3 storage is *incredibly* cheap. You can begin the sign-up process at *https://aws.amazon.com/s3*.

A Real Example

To give you a real example, I use S3 to host the media assets for my blog at *https://www.raymondcamden.com*. (The actual written content is stored in Netlify, which we'll discuss later in the chapter.) I also host a few other small static sites there. My monthly bills over the past year have hovered around 10 to 15 cents.

After signing up, you go into the Amazon Web Services dashboard (Figure 7-1), which can be a bit overwhelming.

Figure 7-1. The Amazon Web Services dashboard

Under Storage and Content Delivery, find S3. S3 groups content into buckets. You can think of them as directories, and generally you'll want a specific bucket for one specific website. Any bucket can become a website, but if you want to use a specific domain, like www.foo.com, then you must name the bucket that domain. In case you're curious, to support both foo.com and www.foo.com, you would create a bucket for foo.com that redirects to the www bucket. Redirects are supported by S3 but won't be covered here. Simply check the documentation (*http://amzn.to/2lvnUGw*) for an example.

To begin, create a new bucket (Figure 7-2). You can name it what you will, but for the book we'll use `orabook.raymondcamden.com`. You won't be able to use the same name, so try using something that includes your own name, or if you have a domain at foo.com, try something like `orabook.foo.com`. For the region, just use US Standard. Depending on your location and your site visitors' location, you may want to select a region that is more specific.

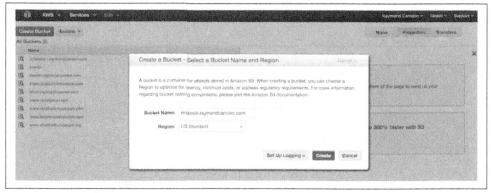

Figure 7-2. Creating a bucket for your site

Immediately you'll see a properties panel open and Static Website Hosting is one of the options. Click to open it (Figure 7-3), and you'll see how easy it is to enable website hosting.

Bucket: orabook.raymondcamden.com   ✕

       Bucket: orabook.raymondcamden.com
       Region: US Standard
Creation Date: Sat Aug 20 09:03:19 GMT-500 2016
       Owner: cfjedimaster

▸ Permissions

▾ Static Website Hosting

You can host your static website entirely on Amazon S3. Once you enable your bucket for static website hosting, all your content is accessible to web browsers via the Amazon S3 website endpoint for your bucket.

Endpoint: orabook.raymondcamden.com.s3-website-us-east-1.amazonaws.com

Each bucket serves a website namespace (e.g. "www.example.com"). Requests for your host name (e.g. "example.com" or "www.example.com") can be routed to the contents in your bucket. You can also redirect requests to another host name (e.g. redirect "example.com" to "www.example.com"). See our walkthrough for how to set up an Amazon S3 static website with your host name.

  ◯ **Do not enable website hosting**

  ◉ **Enable website hosting**

       Index Document: [   ]

       Error Document: [   ]

  ▸ **Edit Redirection Rules:** You can set custom rules to automatically redirect web page requests for specific content.

  ◯ **Redirect all requests to another host name**

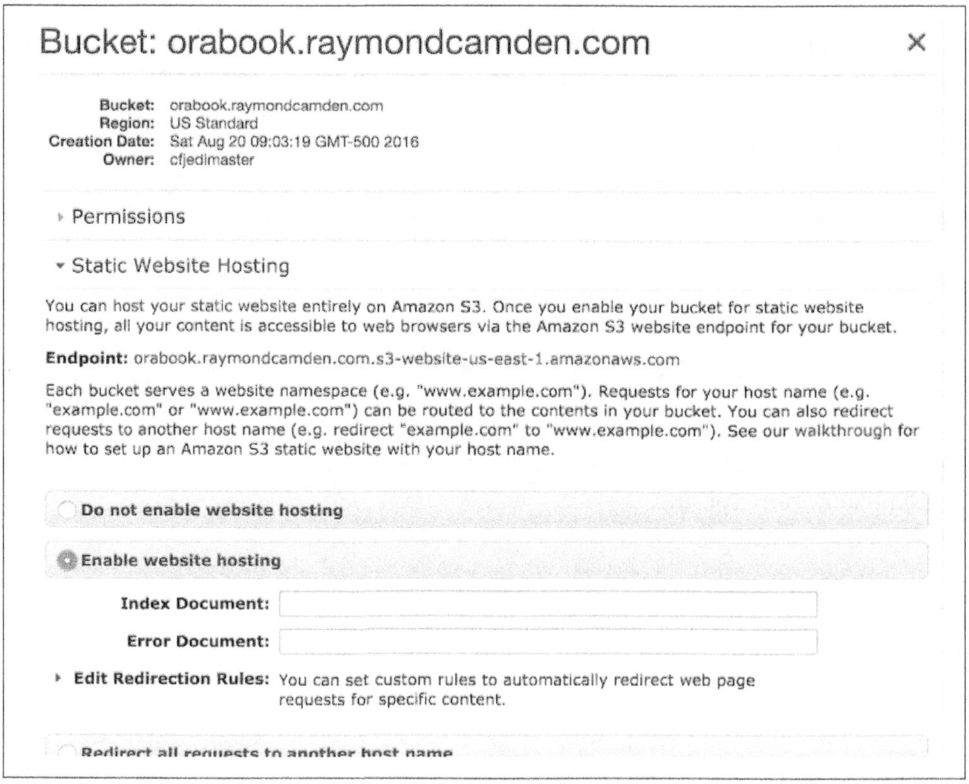

Figure 7-3. Enabling static site hosting

You will need to select an index document. This is simply the document that should be loaded when the site is requested. While you can enter anything here, it is customary to use *index.html*. You can enter an error document as well to be used when a page that doesn't exist is requested (Figure 7-4).

Once you click save, you can try hitting your site using the endpoint that S3 set up for you. In case you missed it, it is in the Static Website Hosting section in Figure 7-3.

Figure 7-4. Your new site, broken

Almost there! You still need to add content to your bucket in order for the site to be displayed. How you get files into S3 is up to you. Most FTP clients support connecting to S3 buckets and that's probably the way you'll want to go, but you can also upload via the S3 web console. Simply use the Upload button and drag and drop files and folders directly into the web page itself. For this demo, I've used the output from the Camden Grounds site created in Chapter 2. You can use any output from the earlier chapters, or simply create a new *index.html* file with some temporary content.

Before you hit upload, you need to modify permissions for the new assets so they are public. Click the Set Details button at the bottom, then click Set Permissions. On that page, check "Make everything public" (Figure 7-5).

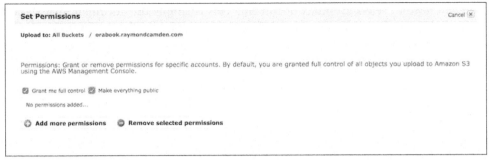

Figure 7-5. Making the assets public

Finally, click Start Upload and the process will begin. Depending on the number and size of the files, it may take a few minutes. The website does a great job of providing feedback as assets are uploaded (Figure 7-6).

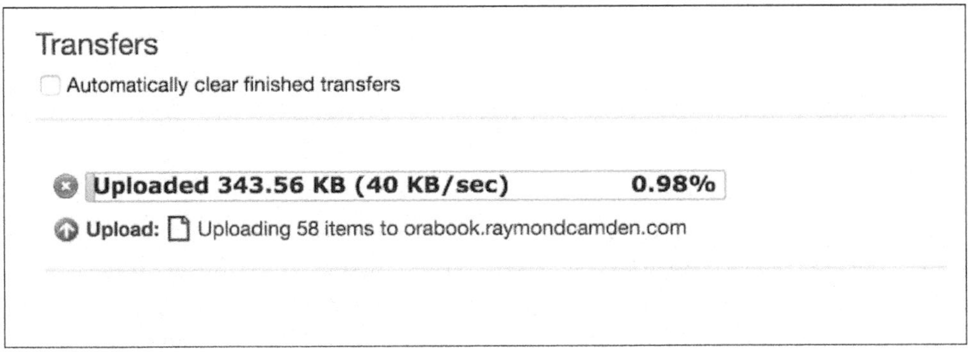

Transfers

☐ Automatically clear finished transfers

⊗ **Uploaded 343.56 KB (40 KB/sec)**   **0.98%**

⬆ **Upload:** 🗋 Uploading 58 items to orabook.raymondcamden.com

Figure 7-6. Upload progress

When done, simply reload the browser with the endpoint URL and you will see your site (Figure 7-7)!

Figure 7-7. Your site is now live!

And that's basically it. The last step is to update the DNS for your domain to point to Amazon. Specifics on that can be found on the Amazon site. Amazon also supports basic redirects. If you migrated from a dynamic site using PHP, for example, you could tell Amazon how to handle requests for those old .php URLs so that visitors don't get errors requesting old URLs.

Hosting a Site on Google Cloud Storage

Working with Google's Cloud Storage system entails a similar process to Amazon. As before, you'll have to sign up at the product page (*https://cloud.google.com/storage*) and provide credit card information. As with S3, prices are very cheap, but I'll repeat the warning. Check the prices carefully so you don't get a surprise at the end of the first billing period. And again, just like S3, Google offers a generous free tier (currently 300 USD for 60 days).

After creating your account, the first thing you need to do (assuming you aren't a Google user already with existing services) is to create a project. You can open up the Project dashboard (*https://console.cloud.google.com/project*) and name it whatever you want. After creating the project, you choose your billing plan. Don't forget you've got $300 of free service for two months, but also don't forget to close the account later if you change your mind.

After you've done this initial work, you can simply open the storage browser (*https://console.cloud.google.com/storage/browser*) to create your bucket. (If this all seems familiar, that's good. It makes moving from S3 to Google, or vice versa, that much easier.)

Go ahead and click "Create a bucket," and give it the same name that we did for Amazon (Figure 7-8). Like with S3, you want your bucket name to match the domain you plan on using, and like S3, it has to be unique. Since we're creating this bucket in the book, you need to pick a different name.

Figure 7-8. Creating the bucket on Google Cloud Storage

Once again, there are multiple ways to upload your files. You can use the web client, but Google also provides a command-line program so let's try that. Go to the Google Cloud SDK page (*https://cloud.google.com/sdk/*) (Figure 7-9) and select the Install link.

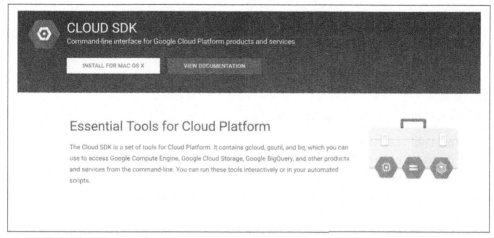

Figure 7-9. The Google Cloud SDK

The SDK Uses

The SDK provides a rich set of tools related to the entirety of Google's Cloud Platform. Everything we've done so far (making a project, creating a bucket) could have been done via the SDK as well. We'll start off by setting permissions for the bucket. We want them to be viewable by the internet as a whole, so we'll use the command line to assign everyone read permission to the bucket.

```
gsutil defacl ch -u AllUsers:R gs://orabook.raymondcamden.com
```

Let's explain what this did.

1. `defacl ch` specifies a change to the default ACL (ACL stands for "access control list" and is a basic way of looking at security for resources).
2. `-u AllUsers:R` specifies everyone ("AllUsers") and the read permission.
3. Finally we specify the bucket. Again, you must change this.

To upload our site, we'll use `gsutil` and the `rsync` command. This will copy everything in one folder up to the bucket. Assuming you're in the folder containing your site, use the following command:

```
gsutil -m rsync -R . gs://orabook.raymondcamden.com
```

Let's break that down argument by argument.

`-m`

Tells the command line to use multiple processes. This is especially handy for an operation that moves a lot of files.

rsync

The actual command we are using in the SDK.

-R

Means to recursively sync all files and folders.

The period

Simply means the current directory.

gs://orabook.raymondcamden.com

The name of the bucket. You *must* change this because your bucket will have a different name.

If you refresh the web client, you'll see your files. What you see here is—obviously—based on what you used for testing. As before, I used the output from the Camden Grounds website (Figure 7-10).

Figure 7-10. The files now show up in the bucket

To test your site, you can use the following URL, with the bucket name in the middle changed of course: *https://storage.googleapis.com/orabook.raymondcamden.com/ index.html.*

There's one really important difference between S3 and Google. The S3 "temp/testing" URL was a root URL. The Google one is a subdirectory under the root domain stor‐ age.googleapis.com. If your static site uses root URLs, such as href="/foo.html", then it will work on S3 but not on Google. This isn't a bug per se, and when you have a real domain pointed to the bucket, it won't matter.

Finally, if you want to get rid of the *index.html* in the URL, go to your bucket and click the little dots at the end to bring up the menu (Figure 7-11):

Figure 7-11. The Buckets menu

Click "Edit website configuration" and in the window that appears (Figure 7-12), enter the main page value. Note you can also specify an error page.

Figure 7-12. Setting website configuration values for the bucket

Deploying with Surge

Cloud-based file storage systems like those from Google and Amazon work great for static websites, but several products now offer tools specifically tailored for static websites and hosting. The list of such products is growing rapidly and in this chapter we'll look at two of them. The first is Surge (*https://surge.sh/*) (Figure 7-13).

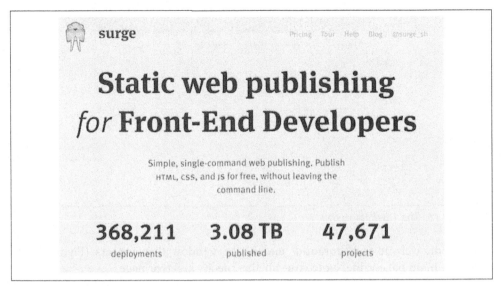

Figure 7-13. The Surge website

Surge is a command-line-only tool for deploying static websites. It offers a free tier that is great for testing and a paid tier that offers additional features. At the time this book was written, the paid tier was $13 a month and included custom SSL and redirects as part of the feature set. You can see more features and pricing on their pricing page (*https://surge.sh/pricing*).

Installing Surge is easy. If you have npm installed, simply run this in your terminal:

```
npm install -g surge
```

Once installed, you can use the `surge` command to deploy a static site. Change directories to any of the outputs from previous chapters, or simply make a new folder with an *index.html* file in it, and then type `surge`. On your first usage of Surge, it will prompt you to log in or create an account (Figure 7-14).

```
→ camdengrounds surge

  Welcome to Surge! (surge.sh)
  Please login or create an account by entering your email and password:

        email: █
```

Figure 7-14. The Surge login/registration

After that, it will prompt you for the directory to deploy (Figure 7-15). It defaults to the current directory.

Figure 7-15. The Surge command line

Simply press the Enter key to accept the default. Next, it will prompt for a domain (Figure 7-16). Notice that it gives you a random domain by default. This is great for testing as you don't have to worry about DNS settings. You can use a real domain name, but for now just accept the temporary domain provided by the command line.

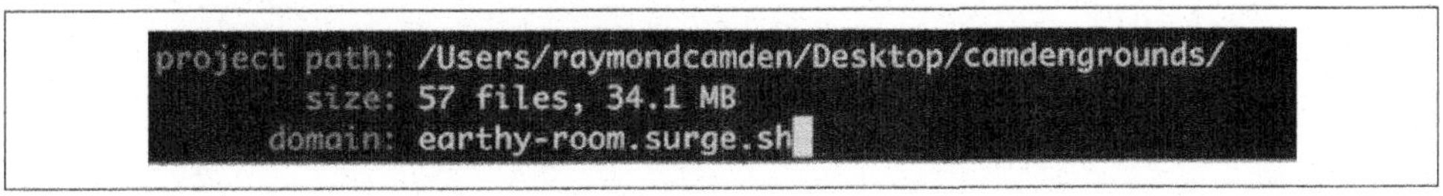

Figure 7-16. The Surge command line

Press the Enter key again, and Surge will begin deploying your site. The command line will provide a simple progress report, and lets you know if it succeeded (Figure 7-17).

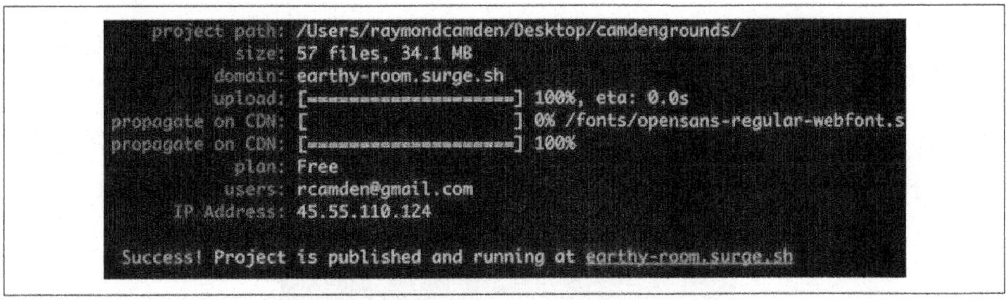

Figure 7-17. Surge has deployed your site

And that's it! Literally seconds after installing Surge, you can have your site up and running for testing purposes. Open your browser to the domain used in the command line and your site will be there. For updates, you'll want to use the same domain name as before. You can either specify the domain at the command line with the -d flag, or provide the directory to deploy the domain as arguments, like so:

```
surge ./ earthy-room.surge.sh
```

Yet another option is to create a file called CNAME that contains the domain name. This file should be in the same directory as your site and will *not* be deployed. Be sure to use only the domain name, like earthy-room.surge.sh, and not the URL. In other words, don't include http://.

Another cool feature of Surge is that it automatically supports "clean" URLs. Any URL that ends in HTML can have the extension left off. For testing, we used the Camden Grounds site from Chapter 2. One of the URLs is the menu. You can see it at *http://earthy-room.surge.sh/menu.html*. But you can also view it at *http://earthy-room.surge.sh/menu*. You'll want to update the links in your HTML, of course, to leave off the HTML.

Surge provides support for custom 404 files by simply looking for a file called *404.html*. If you don't provide one and a visitor requests a file that doesn't exist, you'll get a Surge-branded 404 page (Figure 7-18).

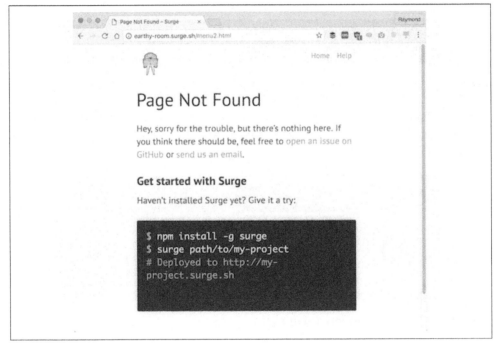

Figure 7-18. The default 404 page

Once you've built and deployed a file called *404.html* like the one in Figure 7-19, Surge will automatically use it when it can't find a requested file.

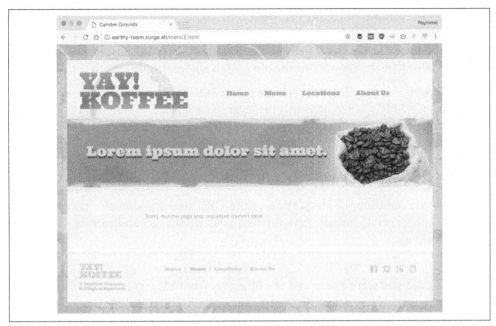

Figure 7-19. A custom 404 page

As you can probably tell, the entirety of Surge is run at the command line. So, for example, if you've forgotten what you've deployed, you can use `surge list` to see your current sites (Figure 7-20).

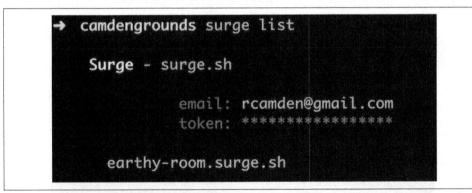

Figure 7-20. Your current list of Surge sites

As another example, if you need to delete a site, you can use the `teardown` command:

```
surge teardown earthy-room.surge.sh
```

So how do premium features work? One of the features you have to pay for is custom URL redirects. Custom redirects allow you to define rules for mapping one URL to another. For example, imagine that you deployed a file called *menyou.html*. Now imagine that you miss this error for months. If you just rename it, then people who bookmarked the old URL will get the 404 page instead. With custom redirects, you can make it so that any request for the old URL is automatically sent to the new one.

Surge supports this by using a special file called ROUTER. (Note that it is all caps like the special CNAME file.) Within this file, every line represents one mapping. A mapping is defined with a status code, an old URL pattern, and a new URL. Status codes can be either 301 ("Moved Permanently") or 307 ("Moved Temporarily"). The following is an example that would fix the problem described above.

```
301 /menyou.html /menu.html
```

Note that you only supply the portion of the URL after the domain name. You can also match a "general" format. Let's say that your site has a subdirectory called blog with URLs like so:

```
http://mysite.com/blog/welcome-to-our-blog.html
```

You've decided you want to rename the directory from blog to news. In order for the old URLs to work, you could either create one entry in ROUTER for every single blog entry, or use a generic pattern like the following:

```
301 /blog/:title /news/:title
```

In this example, `:title` will match any string and be used in the new URL as well.

Once you add a ROUTER file to your project, Surge will recognize this as a premium feature and prompt you to upgrade when you deploy (Figure 7-21).

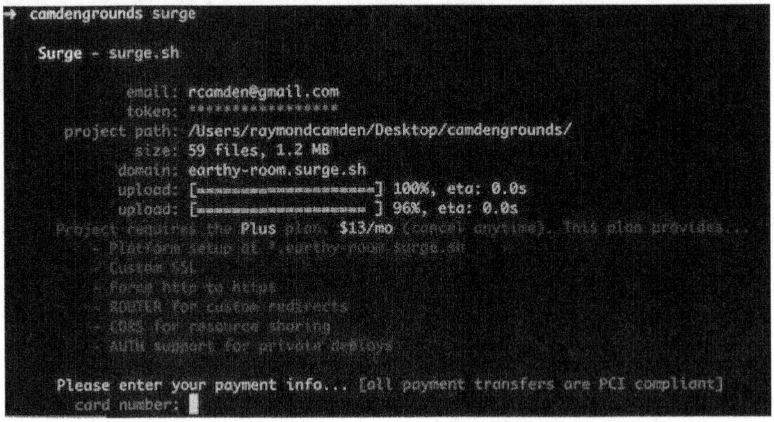

Figure 7-21. Upgrading your Surge site

This is a one-time process. After entering this information, Surge will remember it and won't prompt you again.

Surge is a great, and simple to use, deployment tool for static sites. Be sure to check the Surge website (*https://surge.sh/*) for a complete list of premium features.

Deploying with Netlify

For our next static site publishing and hosting service, we'll take a look at Netlify (*https://www.netlify.com*) (Figure 7-22). Netlify is my favorite static site hosting service and powers my own blog (*https://www.raymondcamden.com*) (which has almost 6,000 blog posts).

Figure 7-22. The Netlify website

Like Surge, Netlify is command-line driven but comes with a web-based dashboard. Currently, Netlify comes with five pricing levels (*https://www.netlify.com/pricing/*). The lowest level is free and should be more than adequate for testing. The "Pro" level (currently $49) is free for open source projects.

Netlify really shines in terms of performance. They use a CDN with multiple endpoints around the planet as well as a speedy DNS and heavy caching. You can also easily add (free) SSL to your site. Netlify has many other features, but my favorite is probably one of the simplest, form handling. We covered this in Chapter 5 using external services, but Netlify has a generic forms-handler built into the service itself. We'll see an example of this later in the chapter.

For a full list of features, see the website (*https://www.netlify.com/features/*), but for now, begin by installing the command line:

```
npm install -g netlify-cli
```

This will install the `netlify` command-line program. Go into your static site (for this example, we'll use The Cat Blog from Chapter 4) and run:

```
netlify deploy
```

Authenticating with Your Browser

The first time you do this, you'll be prompted to authenticate with your browser. This is a one-time process and you can even manage multiple logins if you have to work with different Netlify accounts.

The command line will notice that the site is unknown to the platform and will prompt you to create a new one (Figure 7-23):

```
→ Desktop cd catblog
→ catblog netlify deploy
? No site id specified, create a new site (Y/n)
```

Figure 7-23. Deploying a new site

It will then prompt for the directory to deploy (and, as it defaults to the current directory, you can just press the Enter key).

Netlify will then do its thing (with a nice little progress bar) and, when complete, will give you the URL for your new site (Figure 7-24). Like Surge, it defaults to selecting a random domain for you; obviously, you can use a real domain before going live.

```
→ catblog netlify deploy
? No site id specified, create a new site Yes
? Path to deploy? (current dir)
Deploying folder: /Users/raymondcamden/Desktop/catblog

Deploy is live (permalink):
    http://57c870f56686743d5a35f56c.robber-mousedeer-87783.netlify.com

Last build is always accessible on http://robber-mousedeer-87783.netlify.com
```

Figure 7-24. The site is now deployed

Notice right away something incredibly cool with Netlify. It deployed your site as well as a unique one just for this particular version of the site. Netlify automatically gives you a historical list of views for your content. That means if something goes wrong, you can examine the previous versions to try to nail down when things went haywire.

You can even roll back (via the web admin) to quickly correct the issue. To see that web administrator in action, simply run `netlify open` (Figure 7-25).

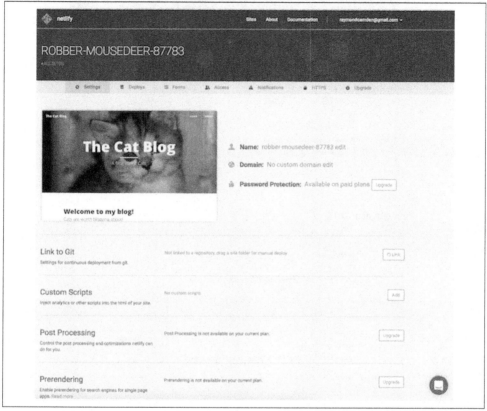

Figure 7-25. Netlify's administrator for your site

Right away, you can see that there's *quite* a bit of information here. Many of the options will require you to upgrade, but you can at least see what's available and decide if they are worth the price. You can see the version history by clicking Deploys. Figure 7-26 shows what it looks like after a second run of the command line.

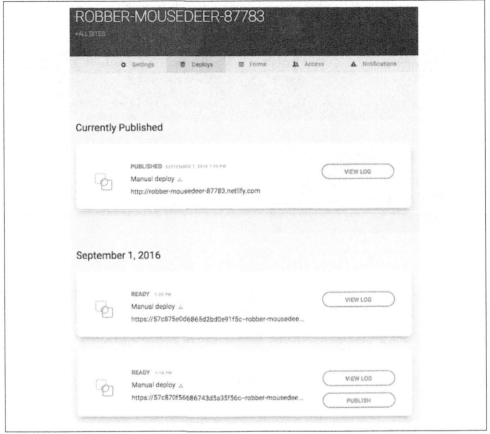

Figure 7-26. Version history for the site

One feature available in the free plans is hooks and notifications. It would be nice if your client could know everytime the site was updated. Click on Notifications → Add Notification → Email notification (see Figure 7-27).

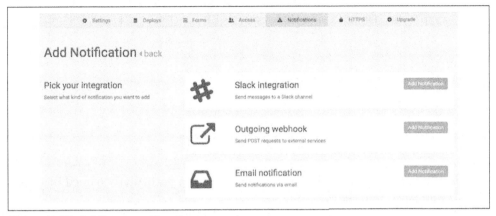

Figure 7-27. Adding a notification

On the next screen, select "Deploy succeeded" for the "Event to listen for" and then enter your email address (Figure 7-28).

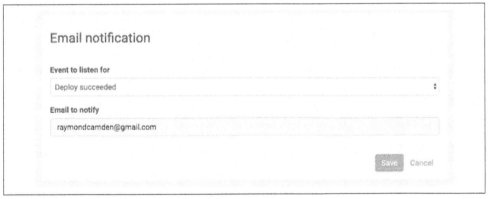

Figure 7-28. Setting up the "Deploy succeeded" notification

Click Save and the notification will be created. Back at the command line, run `net lify deploy` again. When the deploy is complete, you'll get an email notification that includes both the main domain as well as the versioned URL (Figure 7-29).

Figure 7-29. The email notification from Netlify

Another free-tier feature, redirects, is done by using a particularly named file in the root of your site: `_redirects`.

The file should contain one line per redirect with the format being:

```
old path                new path
```

So a real example could look like so:

```
/kats          /cats
```

Your file can also include comments by using a hash sign as the first character:

```
#We thought this spelling would be cute. It wasn't.
/kats          /cats
```

The default HTTP status code is 301, but you can specify another one by adding it to the end of the line.

```
#We thought this spelling would be cute. It wasn't.
/kats          /cats          302
```

And then finally, you can also use "slugs" in the URLs to match specific patterns of URLs.

```
#Old URL for cat adoptions
/adoptions/:year/:breed          /catsneedinghomes/:year/:breed
```

Now that we've looked at some of the free features, let's look at a few of the features available on the paid tier. The easiest one to demonstrate, and one of the most useful features, is automatic form processing. Let's begin by adding a simple contact form to the cat blog we uploaded earlier. The cat blog was created in Chapter 3, and makes use of the Jekyll static site generator. If you skipped that chapter, you may want to quickly read it to get an idea of how it works.

The cat blog used a template ("Clean Blog") that already had a contact form. I literally just took their form and added it to our local Jekyll blog. See Example 7-1.

Example 7-1. The Cat Blog contact form

```
---
layout: page
title: "Contact"
description: "Contact page."
header-img: "img/about-bg.jpg"
---

<p>Please send us your feedback. We care a lot.</p>

<form method="post">
<div class="row control-group">
    <div class="form-group col-xs-12 floating-label-form-group controls">
        <label>Name</label>
        <input type="text" class="form-control" placeholder="Name" id="name"
                required data-validation-required-message=
                    "Please enter your name.">
        <p class="help-block text-danger"></p>
    </div>
</div>
<div class="row control-group">
    <div class="form-group col-xs-12 floating-label-form-group controls">
        <label>Email Address</label>
        <input type="email" class="form-control" placeholder=
          "Email Address" id="email"
                required data-validation-required-message=
                    "Please enter your email address.">
        <p class="help-block text-danger"></p>
    </div>
</div>
<!-- parts deleted -->
<br>
<div id="success"></div>
<div class="row">
    <div class="form-group col-xs-12">
        <button type="submit" class="btn btn-default">Send</button>
    </div>
</div>
</form>
```

To keep the code listing a bit shorter, a few fields were removed. You can find the complete source code in the book's GitHub repository. Note that the form has no action. After generating the static version and deploying to Netlify, you can see the form in action.

If you submit the form, however, you'll get an error (Figure 7-30).

Page Not found

Looks like you've followed a broken link or entered a URL that doesn't
exist on this site.

← Back to our site

Figure 7-30. The form doesn't work quite well yet

Correcting this is incredibly easy. First, add a `netlify` attribute to your form tag:

```
<form method="post" netlify>
```

Then add a proper action to the tag. In this case, we're going to point to a new "thank you" page. (Again, the source of this page may be found on GitHub, but it's just a quick "thank you" message.)

```
<form method="post" action="thankyou" netlify>
```

Don't forget to redeploy the site. Now when you submit the form, you'll be automatically redirected to the "thank you" page. So how do you see your submissions? You've got a couple of options. On the Netlify dashboard for your site, click the Forms tab to see Netilfy's Forms dashboard (Figure 7-31).

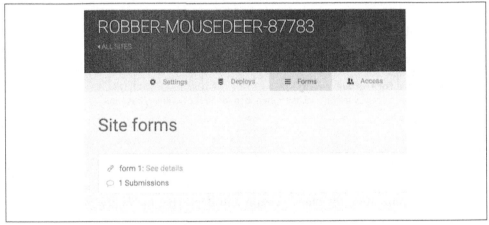

Figure 7-31. Netlify's Forms dashboard

Notice how Netlify refers to the form as "form 1"? You can correct this by adding a name attribute to the form tag:

```
<form method="post" name="Contact Form" action="thankyou" netlify>
```

Now submissions will be labeled correctly (Figure 7-32).

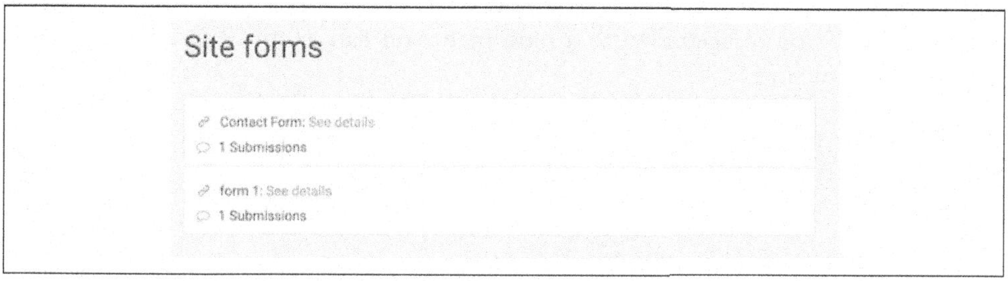

Figure 7-32. How Netlify identifies your form submissions

You can view your form submissions by clicking the Details link in the dashboard, and Netlify provides an API to fetch form results as well, but most likely you simply want to have the submissions sent to you. In your dashboard, go to Notifications and click to add a new Email notification. For the "Event to listen for," select New Form Submission. Notice how the dashboard recognizes the forms you've used. Simply add your email address and save the notification (Figure 7-33).

Figure 7-33. Setting up email notifications for your form

Submit your form again, and in a few moments you'll get an email with the contents of your form (Figure 7-34).

Figure 7-34. Form submissions are now emailed to your account

Finally, let's look at one of the most impressive features of Netlify, automatic processing. On your dashboard, you may have noticed a "Post Processing" section, shown in Figure 7-35. If you've upgraded to a paid plan, you can enable multiple processing options for your site:

Figure 7-35. Setting up post processing for your site

Netlify can automatically perform multiple optimizations for your site's CSS, JavaScript, and images. To be clear, these optimizations are 100% automatic. You literally click a checkbox and, when you deploy, Netlify will optimize what you've asked it to optimize and your users immediately get the benefit. While these are all things you could do yourself, let's be honest—having it done by Netlify while keeping your own code nice and simple is an incredible feature.

How well this works will depend on a few things, of course. In my case, the template used by The Cat Blog had optimized images and mostly optimized CSS and JavaScript already. In my testing, I saw a savings of about 18 KB. This was approximately 5% of the total page load for the home page. Not a huge savings, but for 20 seconds of work on my part, that's a big win. Going forward, as new images and content are added, I can rest assured that Netlify will handle the optimizations for me.

There's quite a bit more to Netlify than we covered here and I encourage you to peruse the docs for a full list of features (*https://www.netlify.com/docs/*). One feature in particular will be of interest to sites with a large or complex review process— deploy contexts. This allows you to deploy different versions of your site with unique settings to allow for previews, QA, and reviews before updating your main site. By connecting your Netlify site to a Git repository, the *entire* publication process can be easily tied to your source control for completely automated updates.

Summary

We hope you can see that moving your static site from a local environment to a live website is a fairly simple process. As static site generators become more popular, you'll see even more options for deployments in the future.

## CHAPTER 8

Migrating to a Static Site

Brian Rinaldi

By this point, we hope that you are thoroughly convinced that creating a static site with one of the many available static site generators is a worthwhile and viable option. Perhaps you are even thinking that it would be the perfect option for an existing CMS site you already maintain, but you're concerned about the complexity of moving all of the site's content to static files.

The good news is that there are lot of solutions for this problem. Although the migration may still be quite a bit of work depending on the size and complexity of your existing site, these migration tools can massively decrease the effort and difficulty.

Of course, all of this depends on two factors: what CMS engine you are coming from and what static site generator you intend to use. Most of the major static site generators have tools to import content from various CMSes, but they don't cover every available option, and some static site generators have many more available importers than others.

Because a lot of factors are involved in this sort of project, in this chapter I'll offer an overview of what might be involved, how some of these importers work, and what available options are out there. We'll cover the static site generators used in this book as well as some others that offer migration options. Let's start off by examining one common scenario.

Migrating from WordPress to Jekyll

Since its introduction in 2003, WordPress has become the most dominant CMS. According to W3Techs (*http://bit.ly/2m8Qn2f*), WordPress is used by 26.8% of the top 10 million websites as determined by Alexa—essentially one-quarter of the entire web runs WordPress. For comparison, the next largest CMS would be Joomla at 2.8%.

Suffice it to say, there's a reasonable chance that, if you are migrating to a static site engine, you are migrating from WordPress. This explains why many static site generators offer a WordPress importer (in fact, many *only* offer a WordPress importer). Let's look at how you might use the importer provided by Jekyll.

Jekyll provides a very comprehensive list of available importers (*https://import.jekyllrb.com/docs/home/*) (24 by my count) from a wide array of CMS and other data formats. All of these run off of Jekyll Import (*https://github.com/jekyll/jekyll-import*) Ruby gem. If you've already installed Jekyll, you already have Ruby Gems installed on your machine, so you can easily install the Jekyll Import gem via the terminal or command prompt.

```
gem install jekyll-import
```

Installing Jekyll

If you haven't installed Jekyll yet, please refer to Chapter 3 for detailed instructions.

Each importer also has their own set of additional dependencies. For instance, the WordPress importer also requires the gems for unidecode (*http://bit.ly/2lD23g4*), sequel (*https://rubygems.org/gems/sequel*), mysql2 (*https://rubygems.org/gems/mysql2*), and htmlentities (*https://rubygems.org/gems/htmlentities*). At this point, you should have Ruby Gems installed, so you should be able to install all of these with one simple command-line statement.

```
gem install unidecode sequel mysql2 htmlentities
```

WordPress on MAMP

A lot of developers (myself included) use MAMP (*https://www.mamp.info/en/*) to run their local WordPress development. As someone who is not really a PHP developer, its option of a one-click install of all of the necessary pieces (MySQL, Apache, PHP) is compellingly simple.

However, MAMP does not come with the full MySQL installation that is necessary to run the WordPress importer for Jekyll. This will cause the gem installation I just described to fail.

After a lot of research and trial and error, I found that the simplest solution was to download and install the full MySQL (*http://www.mysql.com/*). This will not interfere with your MAMP copy of MySQL. Once installed, the gems should install without error.

In order to make the importer use the MAMP copy of MySQL rather than the full MySQL installation, in the configuration (which we will look at in more detail below) you need to point it at the socket for MAMP. For example, on my Mac running macOS El Capitan, the socket was located at `/Applications/MAMP/tmp/mysql/mysql.sock`.

Once everything is installed, you can run the importer, providing the configuration via the command line. The easiest way to do this (in my opinion) is to first copy the configuration from the documentation (*https://import.jekyllrb.com/docs/wordpress/*) into a text editor and edit it there before pasting it into the terminal or command prompt.

Here is the documentation's configuration.

```
ruby -rubygems -e 'require "jekyll-import";
    JekyllImport::Importers::WordPress.run({
        "dbname"        => "",
        "user"          => "",
        "password"      => "",
        "host"          => "localhost",
        "socket"        => "",
        "table_prefix"  => "wp_",
        "site_prefix"   => "",
        "clean_entities" => true,
        "comments"      => true,
        "categories"    => true,
        "tags"          => true,
        "more_excerpt"  => true,
        "more_anchor"   => true,
        "extension"     => "html",
        "status"        => ["publish"]
    })'
```

It's important to note that each of the configuration settings above includes the default value. Thus, if the default value is sufficient for you (for example `"host" => "localhost"`), then you can feel free to remove it.

For example purposes, I'll set up a WordPress variation of my static site samples (*https://github.com/remotesynth/Static-Site-Samples*) example site (Figure 8-1), which is an Adventure Time! fan page. For this example, I don't implement a full copy of the design in WordPress, I'm simply focusing on adding the blog posts.

Figure 8-1. A simple WordPress example site

After creating a new Jekyll site, I open the terminal or command prompt within the Jekyll site folder and run the importer with the configuration as follows:

```
ruby -rubygems -e 'require "jekyll-import";
    JekyllImport::Importers::WordPress.run({
        "dbname"    => "adventuretime",
        "user"      => "root",
        "password"  => "root",
        "socket"    => "/Applications/MAMP/tmp/mysql/mysql.sock",
        "host"      => "localhost",
        "categories"    => true,
        "tags"          => true,
        "extension"     => "html",
        "status"        => ["publish"]
    })'
```

The only thing "out of the ordinary" here is the socket setting, which, as I explained is the sidebar earlier, is necessary in order to connect to the MySQL database running on MAMP (Figure 8-2).

```
●  ●  ●              wp2jekyll — fsevent_watch • jekyll serve — 82×27
...jects/Static-Site-Samples/jekyllsite — -bash ...      ...cts/wp2jekyll — fsevent_watch • jekyll serve      +
^CMCWFHBRRINALD:wp2jekyll brinaldi$ ruby -rubygems -e 'require "jekyll-import";
>     JekyllImport::Importers::WordPress.run({
>       "dbname"   => "adventuretime",
>       "user"     => "root",
>       "password" => "root",
>       "socket" => "/Applications/MAMP/tmp/mysql/mysql.sock",
>       "host"     => "localhost",
>       "comments"        => true,
>       "categories"      => true,
>       "tags"            => true,
>       "extension"       => "md",
>       "status"          => ["publish"]
>     })'
MCWFHBRRINALD:wp2jekyll brinaldi$ jekyll serve
Configuration file: /Users/brinaldi/Documents/projects/wp2jekyll/_config.yml
            Source: /Users/brinaldi/Documents/projects/wp2jekyll
        Destination: /Users/brinaldi/Documents/projects/wp2jekyll/_site
 Incremental build: disabled. Enable with --incremental
        Generating...
                    done in 0.406 seconds.
 Auto-regeneration: enabled for '/Users/brinaldi/Documents/projects/wp2jekyll'
Configuration file: /Users/brinaldi/Documents/projects/wp2jekyll/_config.yml
     Server address: http://127.0.0.1:4000/
   Server running... press ctrl-c to stop.
        Regenerating: 8 file(s) changed at 2016-09-22 16:31:15 ...done in 0.137273 s
econds.
```

Figure 8-2. Running the WordPress importer

As you can see from the image, all eight posts from my sample site are imported as *.html* posts into the *_posts* folder of my Jekyll site (Figure 8-3).

Figure 8-3. A default Jekyll site with the imported WordPress posts

It's important to note that the imported posts are HTML (regardless of the `extension` setting). They also include a ton of metadata added to the Jekyll front matter (*https://jekyllrb.com/docs/frontmatter/*) that is pulled from the WordPress site, including author details and even the WordPress ID. All of these values can be useful when trying to re-create the site as static.

Handling Post Formatting Issues

No automatic import is going to be perfect. There is always going to be some level of manual intervention required.

For instance, during the import discussed here, I did run into some formatting issues that needed to be cleaned up. The WordPress editor allows for (or generates) some technically invalid HTML (for example, `<p><strong></p></strong>`) that the importer doesn't handle. This can be handled prior to export by running post code through an HTML formatter (like DirtyMarkup) or after export by manually editing the affected posts.

Another consideration is the use of shortcodes (*https://en.support.wordpress.com/shortcodes/*), which are common in WordPress. Since the converter has no way of knowing the shortcodes, these will have to be handled manually as well. The complexity of this task obviously depends on how frequently your sites used shortcodes in post content.

Nonetheless, even accounting for these sorts of issues, using the importer could potentially save you a lot of time when moving from WordPress to Jekyll.

Other Migration Options

Jekyll has the most exhaustive list of import tools, but other static site engines also offer some.

Hugo

Hugo (*https://gohugo.io/*) offers importers from CMS such as WordPress and Drupal, blog hosting services such as Blogger and Tumblr, and even other static site generators like Jekyll and Octopress (a Jekyll-based tool).

Let's take a really quick look at how to use the WordPress migration tools for Hugo. The nice part about this tool is that it is actually built as a plugin for WordPress, which makes the installation relatively simple.

First, download the code from the GitHub repository (*http://bit.ly/2lDaHeq*) by clicking the "Clone or Download" button and choosing Download Zip. Unzip the file and place the unzipped folder in your WordPress */wp-content/plugins* directory. If you go to your site's admin, you should now see the plugin listed under plugins. Go ahead and activate it (Figure 8-4).

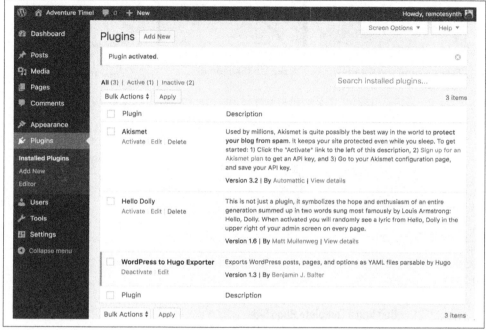

Figure 8-4. The WordPress to Hugo exporter plugin activated

Once activated, you should have an "Export to Hugo" option under your Tools menu. Selecting that will download a zip file containing the posts, pages, and files you'll need to copy into Hugo.

Assuming that you have a new Hugo site already set up, you can simply copy the contents of the export `post` folder into your Hugo site's `content` folder. All your posts should be there, converted nicely into Markdown.

Another nice feature of the plugin is that it also includes the images and uploads from your WordPress site's *wp-content/uploads* folder. You can place this inside the `static` folder under your Hugo site to access any images and uploads from your new content.

This allowed me to easily add the thumbnail metadata for the Robust (*https://github.com/dim0627/hugo_theme_robust*) Hugo theme to the front matter for my posts as:

```
thumbnail: "wp-content/uploads/2016/09/wakeup.jpg"
```

And added back in my header images for my sample Adventure Time! site (Figure 8-5).

Figure 8-5. My sample site after importing it into Hugo displayed using the Robust theme

Building a Complete Hugo Site

For more detailed instructions on working with Hugo, please refer back to Chapter 4 which explains how to build a complete documentation site using Hugo.

Middleman

Middleman (*https://middlemanapp.com/*) is a very popular Ruby-based static site generator. Unfortunately, Middleman does not maintain an official list of migration tools, though there is a WordPress-to-Middleman conversion tool (*https://github.com/mdb/wp2middleman*) (there are guides for other CMSes, but I was unable to locate any other tools).

The importer is available as a Ruby gem (as is Middleman). So, first, install the tool:

```
gem install wp2middleman
```

From within your WordPress site, go to Tools → Export to perform a standard export of all content into a WordPress XML file. Next, open the terminal or command prompt in the folder where you have the export XML and run the tool. For example, with an export file named adventuretime.wordpress.2016-10-11.xml, I ran:

```
wp2mm adventuretime.wordpress.2016-10-11.xml
```

This generated a folder named export that contained all of the WordPress posts as Markdown with front matter ready for Middleman.

Hexo

Hexo (*https://hexo.io/*) is a popular JavaScript-based static site generator that runs on Node.js. Hexo lists a number of migration tools in its plugins directory (*https://hexo.io/plugins/*). These include migrators for WordPress (*https://github.com/hexojs/hexo-migrator-wordpress*), Blogger (*https://github.com/hr6r/hexo-migrator-blogger*), and Joomla (*https://github.com/welksonramos/hexo-migrator-joomla*), as well as from a standard RSS feed (*https://github.com/hexojs/hexo-migrator-rss*), which means you can import from most any CMS that has an RSS output.

Harp

As covered in Chapter 2, Harp is a JavaScript-based static site generator. It does not maintain an official list of migration tools, but the community has created some, including one for importing from WordPress (*https://github.com/EdgeCaseBerg/wpJson4Harp*) and another for importing from Jekyll (*https://github.com/edrex/jekyll2harp*). It is worth noting that the WordPress importer requires that it be configured in Python.

Building a Site with Harp

If you're interested in learning how to build a basic static site using the Harp engine, please refer back to Chapter 2.

Many More Options Are Available

Obviously, we cannot cover every available option here. The important thing to take away from this is that these tools do exist, though for the most part, they are built and maintained by the user community of whichever static site generator you choose. Assuming one exists that suits your needs, it's certainly worth trying as it might save hours of work doing a manual migration, and makes the move to a static site that much more compelling.

Go Forth and Be Static

We hope that this book has given you a solid understanding of the static site generator ecosystem and the tools and skills necessary to build your first static site (or move your existing dynamic site to static). Perhaps you'd heard a lot about static site generators but were concerned that you'd give up too much by going that route. But the simplest solution to a problem is generally the best solution. So, if your site fits well with a static solution, why not get the added benefits of speed, security, and flexibility that they offer?

One thing that should be clear is that this ecosystem is growing and changing very quickly. New static site generators are created, existing ones are updated, and new third-party tools get introduced at a rapid pace. While this can seem intimidating, it represents a fast-growing community for a solution that is gaining more acceptance and usage every day.

As this book has shown, there are already a lot of mature and trustworthy solutions in the ecosystem, and getting started with them really isn't that difficult. So there's no need to hesitate—dive right in and go static!

Index

web servers, 141
DirtyMarkup, 174
Disqus, 101-106, 111
documentation sites, 4, 69-86
    challenges of static site generators with, 69
    characteristics of, 69
    creating with Hugo (see Hugo)
    DocWeb for, 72
    generator choices for, 70
    language specification in, 71-73
    scrolling navigation, 85
documentation, single-page, 73
DocWeb, 72, 79
    scrolling navigation and, 85
Drupal, 86, 174
dynamic element additions, 87-111
    comments, 101-106
    forms, 87-101
    search, 106-111

E

EJS (Embedded JavaScript), 12, 15-16
    partial function in, 18
Eventbrite, 111

F

Facebook Comments, 101
feed.xml, 49
file-based data formats, 5
Firebase, 111
flexibility, 3
Forestry.io, 136-137
forms, 87-101
    adding to demo site, 99-101
    automatic form processing, 162, 165
    Formspree, 97-101
    Google Docs Forms, 93-97
    Wufoo, 88-93
Formspree, 97-101
front matter, 41, 46, 78, 79
FullCalendar, 111

G

getting started guides, 73
Ghost, 86
GitHub, 122
GitHub Pages, 39, 66
GitHub style code fences, 76

global data, 19-21
globals key, 19
Go Template, 80
Google Calendar, 111
Google Cloud SDK, 149
Google Cloud Storage, 147-151
Google Custom Search Engine (CSE), 106-111
Google Docs Forms, 93-97
Google Static Maps API, 32
Grunt, 141
Gulp, 141

H

Handlebars, 5, 127
Harp, 10-37, 177
    basics, 12-16
    client-side routing support, 37
    _contents folder, 37
    CSS/JavaScript preprocessing, 37
    current variable, 28
    data in, 19-25
    dynamic pages, 29-37
    dynamic templates, 21-25
    environment variable, 37, 100
    example site build, 25-37
    generating a site, 25
    harp server, 13
    installing, 10-12
    layouts, 16-17
    partials, 17-19
    path value, 28
    source value, 28
    static output creation, 25
    underscores in file names, 19
    yield variable, 28
harp server, 22
headless CMS, 139
Hexo, 122, 122, 139, 177
home page, 35-37
Homebrew, 74
hosting, 3
HTML formatters, 174
HTML preprocessors, 12
Hugo, 70-86
    adding content with, 77-79
    BaseURL value, 80
    buildDrafts flag, 85
    --buildDrafts flag, 83
    categories value, 79, 82

categories_weight value, 79, 82
changing draft status, 83
code highlighting, 76-77
command-line utility, 75
date value, 78
and DatoCMS, 139
documentation, 86
draft value, 78
front matter, 78, 79
initial file generation, 75
installation, 74-75
layout creation with, 79-85
.LinkTitle, 83
migrating to WordPress, 174-176
$name value, 82
.Pages, 83
pipes, 82
prebuilt themes, 73
range keyword, 82
script tags in, 81
site configuration with, 76-77
.Site.Taxonomies.categories variable, 82
site.title variable, 80
syntax highlighting documentation, 77
$taxonomy value, 82, 83
title value, 78
tool for Contentful, 139
urlize, 83

I

IIS, 141
includes, 80
informational sites, 4

J

Jade, 5, 12, 14, 18
JavaScript preprocessors, 12
Jekyll, 39-67, 70, 174, 177
    additional files, 52-54
    automatic pagination, 66
    available importers, 170
    blog templates, 60-61
    categories value, 47
    changing post from HTML to Markdown, 65
    CMS and (see CloudCannon)
    collections, 66
    _config.yml file, 44, 57, 62
    Contact page, 45

content management with (see Jekyll Admin)
content variable, 50
converters, 86
customization, 59-66
data files, 54-57
_data folder, 54
date value, 46
and DatoCMS, 139
default site, 43
description text, 64
Disqus with, 105
documentation, 49
error message from template, 60
file naming, 45
folders and files created by, 44-45
generating site, 59
GitHub Pages, 66
header image, 63
include command, 51-52
installation, 40
jekyll s, 42
jekyll serve, 42
layout value, 46
layouts and includes, 50-52
Liquid, 48-50
migration from WordPress, 169-174
Netlify CMS and, 122
new site creation, 41-45
permalink value, 54, 58
plugin system, 66
port value, 58
post excerpt value, 49
site configuration, 57-59
site.title variable, 52
socket setting, 172
theme files, 44
title value, 52, 58
underscores in file names, 45
URL components, 47
writing posts in, 45, 48
YAML formatting, 46
Jekyll Admin, 130-135
    setup, 131
    site editing, 131-135
Joomla, 177
JSON, 5, 78

About the Authors

Raymond Camden is a Developer Advocate for IBM. His work focuses on the StrongLoop platform, Bluemix, hybrid mobile development, Node.js, HTML5, and web standards in general. He's a published author and presents at conferences and user groups on a variety of topics. Raymond can be reached at his blog (*https://www.raymondcamden.com/*), @raymondcamden (*https://twitter.com/raymondcamden?*) on Twitter, or via email at *raymondcamden@gmail.com*.

Brian Rinaldi is the Developer Programs Manager at Progress Software focused on ensuring that the developer relations team creates top-notch content for the web development community on the Progress Software Developer Network. Brian also serves as co-editor of *Mobile Web Weekly* (*http://mobilewebweekly.co/*) and authored a report on Static Site Generators for O'Reilly. You can follow Brian via @remotesynth (*https://twitter.com/remotesynth?*) on Twitter or on his blog (*http://remotesynthesis.com*).

Colophon

The animals on the cover of *Working with Static Sites* are gooseneck barnacles (*Pollicipes pollicipes*) and also go by the names goose barnacles or stalked barnacles. They are an edible crustacean and considered a delicacy in Portugal and Spain where they're known as *percebes*.

Gooseneck barnacles can be found near the oceans' surface, attached to rocks or other hard exteriors. They are filter-feeders and rely on the ocean's motion to provide sustenance. They feed on algae and other vegetation, but are also known to consume copepods and brine shrimp.

Being hermaphroditic allows gooseneck barnacles to reproduce easily as long as they are set close to one another, and breeding takes place over eight months of the year, beginning in the warmer months of 50 to 60 degrees Fahrenheit weather. Once the fertilized eggs (in batches of 100,000 to 250,000) have been incubated for about 30 days, they are released as free swimming larva.

It was once believed that barnacle geese actually spawned from gooseneck barnacles because geese migration had not yet been discovered and therefore, no one had witnessed the barnacle geese's mating cycles. Because of this belief, eating barnacle geese on traditionally Christian days of fasting from meat was generally allowed in European countries.

Many of the animals on O'Reilly covers are endangered; all of them are important to the world. To learn more about how you can help, go to *animals.oreilly.com*.

The cover image is from *Pictorial Museum of Animated Nature*. The cover fonts are URW Typewriter and Guardian Sans. The text font is Adobe Minion Pro; the heading font is Adobe Myriad Condensed; and the code font is Dalton Maag's Ubuntu Mono.

Learn from experts.
Find the answers you need.

Sign up for a **10-day free trial** to get **unlimited access** to all of the content on Safari, including Learning Paths, interactive tutorials, and curated playlists that draw from thousands of ebooks and training videos on a wide range of topics, including data, design, DevOps, management, business—and much more.

Start your free trial at:
oreilly.com/safari

(No credit card required.)

CPSIA information can be obtained
at www.ICGtesting.com
Printed in the USA
BVOW11s0324100317

478111BV00003B/4/P